CALL TO ACTION

Many of us want to respond to the questions 'What sort of society do we want?' and 'What sort of people do we need to be to achieve it?' These the Archbishops of Canterbury and York have asked us to explore over the next few years. Yet some of us have felt that there is nothing we can do in our own neighbourhood to affect the future of our nation.

This book asks: What sort of a neighbourhood do we want? How do we achieve it? It then goes on to say what a small group of ordinary people can do in their own community, and offers at least forty suggestions for practical action which can start in anyone's family, job, street, church and community life. It provides a programme of study and action for Christian house groups, and suggests that Christians see their role in society as contributing something essential and distinctive for a healthy society —yeast in the dough of the wider community.

Michael Wright, Vicar of Ormesby, a large urban parish in Middlesbrough, and formerly a country parish priest, was before being ordained a professional journalist. He is an Associate Member of the British Institute of Management and writes and lectures on parish management practice.

Call to Action

MICHAEL WRIGHT

MOWBRAYS
LONDON & OXFORD

© A. R. Mowbray & Co Ltd 1977

ISBN 0 264 66378 0

First published 1976
by A. R. Mowbray & Co Ltd
The Alden Press, Osney Mead
Oxford OX2 OEG

Text set in 10/10½pt Baskerville
and printed in Great Britain
by Richard Clay (The Chaucer Press), Ltd,
Bungay Suffolk

Contents

For JOHN, JILL and ANGELA

Acknowledgements

I WANT to pay tribute to the interest, ideas, encouragement and support of the members of St Cuthbert's Church, Ormesby which have helped this book along. The writing has only been done because of the encouragement of my wife, and the kindness of Mr and Mrs M. Jarratt who provided a quiet place far from the telephone bell where I was able to write it, and the willing co-operation of my colleagues at St Cuthbert's the Reverend Sugu Chandy and Deaconess Marjorie Brook.

Introduction

We can find fresh hope and vision through many small groups of people, who are concerned about the way society is going, and who meet regularly, talk and sift ideas, and search for some clearer understanding of our problems and some constructive ideas for tackling them. Lord Clark in his book *Civilisation* writes: 'It is lack of confidence more than anything else that kills a civilisation. We can destroy ourselves by cynicism and disillusion, just as effectively as by bombs.'

As a former journalist, I am well aware that our current fashion in news presentation and investigation journalism breeds cynicism and disillusion. The counter attack on our national malaise can only come through small groups of people in neighbourhoods, villages, social centres, and places of work, who are searching for some vision of life as it could and should be, and who are determined to do something in their own small sphere of influence towards achieving that vision.

A vision is needed, for 'without vision the people perish' (Proverbs 29.18). A vision grows from basic convictions about the meaning and purpose of human life. Powerful forces have grown up in recent years each pushing for their particular vision of life, whose prime concern seems to be either the creation of wealth, or the distribution of wealth. Christians have been given a vision of life based on the prime importance

11

of our humanity, we are children of God, with a capacity for love, fellowship, spirituality, creativity, goodness, industry, selflessness and nobility of character, and a responsibility to work for justice, for truth, and health for everyone of body, mind and spirit.

This vision will only come into operation as it is talked about, challenged, and related to specific action that we can take in the complex life we all live now. There are no simple 'Christian answers' to our personal and national problems, but from a deep understanding of the teaching of Christ and the implications that flow from that teaching, we can find our way towards 'life in all its fulness' (John 10.10) which is what he said he came to bring.

If, in every neighbourhood, some of the themes dealt with in this book, are taken seriously by Christians in discussion with other people, whether Christian or not, then we can all begin to understand, work for, and achieve the sort of society we want, and learn to be the sort of people we need to be if we are to achieve it.

I

WE CAN MOVE
MOUNTAINS

THE Call to the Nation by the Archbishops of Canterbury and York in October 1975 was to the nation as a whole, not just to the churches nor just to the Church of England. It is clearly important for anyone, whatever their beliefs and convictions, to face the two basic questions the Archbishops put to the nation:

What sort of society do we want?
What sort of people do we need to be to achieve it?

It is also important to face a third question:

How do we achieve the sort of society we want?

This book is intended as a guide and stimulator to help ordinary people, who have Christian convictions, to see the possibilities for doing something positive in their local neighbourhood. This is an activists book, written from the conviction that applied faith really can move mountains. *We* can move mountains. By 'we' I mean ordinary people with no special qualifications or expertise, who simply feel very concerned to do something worthwhile to help create a better society for our children and grandchildren to grow up in.

Some people will write books about the national malaise and the things top people need to do to put us on the right road; other people may write books about the Archbishops' questions from a secular viewpoint. This book does neither. It is written from the basis of Christian faith, and it is written not for the national scene, but for the local neighbourhood. Faith, prayer, conviction, determination, courage and willpower are qualities of mind and personality that can change society. Each one of us may not have much faith or courage or willpower, but it is surprising and impressive what even a small group of people can achieve when they band together on a common objective.

An all-too-common thread that runs through so many of the 27,000 letters written to the Archbishop of Canterbury by ordinary people from all parts of Britain, and I read quite a few of them, is that the ordinary person can do nothing on his own to create a better society. Two quotations included in John Poulton's book *Dear Archbishop* (Hodder & Stoughton 60p) are typical of many, many more in those letters:

'Unlike yourself (the Archbishop of Canterbury) I am powerless to make even a small ripple in the "river of life" which seems to flow faster, caring little which way it twists and turns' (p. 31).
'What can I do about all this? It is like trying to swim in suet pudding' (p. 33).

Certainly one individual, working alone, and trying to change the whole of society, will find the task rather like trying to swim in suet pudding. On the other hand, every great movement in history which has brought about important changes which affect the whole of society has started in a small way, in a local neighbourhood, from a small gathered group of people, who more often than not simply had their sights on changing something in their own local area. In time the movement strengthened, grew and extended its influence widely.

The Christian Church grew in this way, and developments within it like the Franciscan movement, the Reformation and the Methodist movement in England all grew in this way too. But on a more limited scale and at the present time, we can see that from the activities of a small group of discriminating beer drinkers wanting pubs in their own neighbourhood to return to hand pumps and wooden beer barrels has grown the Campaign for Real Ale. In less than three years it has become a national movement with many successes. There are many other examples of the same pattern.

A small group of people, reacting against current trends, and taking action together in their own neighbourhood, can in many cases surprise themselves and the nation by the influence they eventually can come to exert in their chosen field of concern. The current debate about society is one in which small groups of people in each neighbourhood have a real chance of influencing. It is certainly not a case for people to just sit back and assume that powers beyond our control are going to govern and change our lives without us having a say in the matter.

This book offers suggestions for action, and ways of implementing the action. It may be that in time, the current practice by Christians of one or more denominations meeting together in small groups in one another's houses for friendship, discussion, study, prayer and corporate action may come to be recognised as a powerful and widespread adult educational movement with a potential power to really influence the whole of society deeply. Perhaps the house group movement may in its turn be even more influential in time than the Sunday School movement which Robert Raikes founded in his Gloucestershire village, and which came to play a very important role in the whole religious and moral outlook of England.

At present the danger is that too many Christian groups are just introverted talking shops, in which the problems of a situation can be endlessly explored, then nothing done about them. The Chinese have a proverb, 'A journey of a thousand miles must begin with one step.' That first important step, which can lead to so many more, must be taken from where you stand right now. The sum of all the little constructive steps taken in each neighbourhood will be a great leap forward nationally.

This book looks at various aspects of local community life, and offers at least forty specific suggestions for Christian people to consider in responding to the Archbishops' questions. Other themes and concerns are likely to emerge from the House Group Discussion Programme on this book which is offered in the final chapter. The particular suggestions will help any group from being just a talking shop, by keeping the theme of action, specific local action by members of that group, always on the agenda. *The specific suggestions are numbered, and printed in italic print in the text.*

PROBLEMS OF PROGRESS

THE Archbishops of Canterbury and York have asked us what sort of society we want. Most of us like many of the things we have at present. As we are all rather conservative and don't like things changing too much, most replies to that question tend to be that we want the sort of society we already have, but with some improvements. After all, we have a lot to be thankful for.

In modern Britain we have a high standard of living. The vast majority of people live in good houses, are warm, well fed, have jobs and the chance to enjoy their leisure. There are luxury goods in the shops, we have entertainment in our homes through television and radio, we have information about the world around us. There are plenty of places to go for leisure activities especially if you own a car, as so many people do. Education is freely available from the age of five to fifteen years, and beyond that for the academically able. There is wide choice in our shops of food, clothes, and things to make our homes comfortable and attractive.

Modern technology has given us a whole range of labour-saving devices for our homes and places of work. We have a Welfare State organised to ensure that the poor, the sick, the elderly and the inadequate are cushioned from the effects of their disability. So many diseases of the past have been conquered, and we can now expect to live longer, grow taller and fatter than our forefathers, and when we are ill modern medicine can cure so many of the things doctors in previous generations could do nothing about at all. You can even have a new heart if you need one.

Science has taken men to the moon and back and in so many ways is extending the limits of human knowledge. Any young man or woman with ability and determination can, with luck, achieve the highest political, scientific, managerial or artistic heights irrespective of which family they were born into, or which school they went to.

The list of achievements of which many people are so proud is almost endless. The bewildering thing is that in spite of all these improvements, our society is a society of many problems, deep anxieties and an unending stream of complaints and grumbles. Politicians, parsons, union and management leaders, teachers, parents, citizens, Old Uncle Tom Cobley and all join in the business of trying to put the world to rights by pointing out in discussions and speeches what is wrong. Documentary programmes on television and radio, and feature articles in newspapers and magazines feed us constantly with the ailments and inadequacies of our society today.

Time and again the solutions they suggest are either still materialistic—better wages, buildings or a more efficient administration and stronger measures to outlaw anti-social behaviour—or they urge people to behave more responsibly. They do not usually suggest *how* we can persuade people to be more responsible. Conscience, which can be a stern internal authority guiding and indeed ruling a person's behaviour and self-control, is not something which you relate just to public opinion. It is more personal and internal, related to God and religious teaching, and a sense of what we 'ought' to do. If popular opinion drops God out of the picture, then conscience and the force of internal self-discipline will be weakened considerably. The drive to higher human conduct is one of response to a Higher Being, not a higher standard of living.

MATERIAL PROSPERITY: SPIRITUAL POVERTY

In the last hundred years all sorts of folk have been

busy building the brave new world, on the assumption that material progress is the only real progress. Science and industry have combined in shaping a philosophy of materialism. The assumptions about human life and behaviour have been based on theories that deny that the human mind is anything more than the physical operation of chemical substances in living organs. This reduces God and spirituality to self-delusions, morals to the inhibitions and repressions of traditional societies, and the needs of people simply to a job, family, friends, a comfortable modern home, personal freedom, leisure and entertainment. A sick person therefore can be treated by chemistry, a problem community by slum clearance and rehousing, and society's problems by better education, information and freedom to make their views known. Responsible and moral behaviour has changed and now virtually amounts to socially organised hedonism. We have to seriously examine what is wrong with that philosophy for we find nowadays we have come to a painful economic, social and spiritual crisis.

In many cities, even where houses and schools are modern and pleasant, most people have jobs, and basic medical needs are easily available, more and more people are frightened by the growing sense of aggression, violence and vandalism in the neighbourhood and at work. A wide range of constructive leisure time opportunities are threatened either by misuse or by neglect.

Endless are the grumbles about poor workmanship, slovenly behaviour, bad service and a 'couldn't care less' attitude. The standards of conscientiousness, service to others and self-discipline appear to so many people to be in steep decline. The 1976 report of the Chief Inspector of Constabulary shows a deeply disturbing rise in crime, violence and general dishonesty.

We cannot get away from the fact that the ideals that inspire behaviour, shape a culture, and impose limits on what we think it right to do, have to be rooted in what we believe human life is for, and to whom we

19

are accountable for our actions. Self-discipline, conscientiousness and satisfaction from a job well done are not automatic qualities in human nature. Human beings have evolved over many millions of years, through long stages of animal behaviour, and civilised human life is something we can recognise only in the last few thousand years. The inner springs of socially acceptable behaviour, culture, good manners, godliness and goodness are a veneer laid on a deep layer of basically selfish behaviour. Our religion with its focus upon a sense of awe, love, fear, gratitude and service to God has imposed upon us disciplines to restrict within ourselves the baser human attitudes, and has encouraged us in attitudes and actions which Christ taught.

What is disturbing now is that our whole generation may be moving away from the social, moral and cultural security of religious faith, and that this will be very harmful to the wellbeing of us all. A generation of children is growing up whose spiritual training has been virtually ignored. It is among this generation that we now have such an alarming rise in criminal behaviour, as the Metropolitan Police Commissioner, and the Chief Constables of the English counties show us in their reports over the last five years.

So many of these youngsters have virtually no sense of guilt or conscience, and many show evidence of being largely ignored at home as they have grown up. They have been well fed, and given both money and freedom, but very little discipline or teaching at home about faith and life. Every child needs to be taught by his parents about God, and be given an experience of both love and discipline, so that he grows up with the springs of self-discipline inside him with a conscious reference to God.

THE MIDAS TOUCH
Modern thought will have to re-examine its completely materialistic dogma in trying to give us a full account of life, behaviour and spirituality, for the weaknesses of

social and political ideals which are simply materialistic are being highlighted. We now face new social and spiritual problems that are being created by our wealth, our comfort, and our philosophy of life. They are not problems that can be solved by unlimited growth; they are problems created by our ability to use technology and create the most amazing things, because we know how and because we can raise the money to produce them if we can be reasonably sure of selling them.

We have grown accustomed to justifying our behaviour on the grounds of 'We can afford it,' 'It is cost-effective,' and to stop doing certain things because they are uneconomic. The big question we must now face is 'Ought we to do this?' We must look for moral principles that will be appropriate for guiding our behaviour and our civilisation.

For instance, we can make a cup of tea quite easily with a spoonful of tea leaves in a teapot. Technology allows us to put that spoonful into a neatly sealed little paper bag and make our cup of tea with a teabag. It is very convenient. I just wonder how many trees each year are being used up making tea bags, that are really quite unnecessary. Newspaper reports tell us that we are using up the world's wood supply more rapidly than we can replace it. The cost of our newspapers has gone up in the last couple of years, due among other things to the rising cost of newsprint. Newsprint costs more partly because there is less of it. I wonder how much of the scarcity is due to diverting supplies of wood to odd extra 'conveniences' like teabags.

Our business civilisation puts money values before all else, and says that while social responsibilities are very nice they are often too expensive to accept unless the government passes a law to compel everyone to take heed of them. The values of the business civilisation amount to what is 'cost effective', and if you can make a bigger profit by putting spoonsful of tea into bags, as well as selling tea by the quarter pound packet, then good luck to you and go ahead. The element of long-term social benefit has to take second place to the freedom of an individual or company to do their own thing.

What we now know about the limits of the earth to sustain our demands on it, and our treatment of it, such practices have something of the touch of King Midas about them. Midas was the king who dreamed of prosperity, grandeur and luxury. Granted one wish, he asked that everything he touched might turn to gold. It did. The things he touched of course included his food, his clothing and his friends.

Henry Ford's bright idea to make cars cheaply by putting all the pieces together on an assembly line meant every worker had the same job to do over and over again. The chap who had to tighten the same six nuts on every car that came past him every few minutes became very efficient at his task. The system produced a lot of cars, and set the pattern of production for a wide range of goods throughout the world. It has made a lot of profit, and used up a lot of materials. It started out to meet the demand for cars; it now creates a demand for cars. People need to be kept employed, cars are made more flimsy, so you need to buy another one as soon as possible. It has created a boring and soul destroying pattern of work, which takes away any real chance of pride and satisfaction in the job done. Customers talk of a new car being a 'Friday afternoon product', when the assembly-line workers were bored stiff. There seems little to choose morally between the serfdom of the lowest classes in the Middle Ages, and the serfdom of the assembly-line system today.

Another result of the mass production method is that it has made 'uneconomic' many craft skills in which workers could take a real pride in their achievements. Nowadays we think of mass production as inevitable, but perhaps if different ideals had motivated people in the past, a less affluent but more creative style of production could have been developed.

As well as business criteria shaping our culture and values, science has shaped them too. Scientists have explored, observed and reported the world about us. In doing so they have normally excluded from their work a moral principle. Science, they say, is morally neutral, it is the skill of impartial observation and analysis. So the way the chemist observes the action of two chemicals put together in a jar has been used too to observe the way people or animals behave. The aim is to form an unbiased assessment and understanding of what is happening.

Impartial observation, and free enterprise, are two principles that have produced a great deal of knowledge, wealth and benefit to our society, but we are now beginning to realise how spiritually impoverished these two principles are. They have joined hands in our generation to become the central themes of our culture. 'What do people want?'—'Then let's supply it.' 'It is not our job to decide whether this is good or bad if enough people want it.' 'Who is to judge what is right or wrong? It all depends on the individual, the circumstances, and how he or she feels about it.' Moral neutrality has become a guiding principle in so many aspects of life. As a new found freedom from the constraints of 'old-fashioned morality' it seemed a breath of fresh air coming into life not so many years ago. Intellectually it is respectable because it accords to each individual the right and the responsibility of making up his or her own mind, but it is foolish not to recognise that human beings in groups have their behaviour directed by group norms. A group morality may to some be restrictive and irksome, but will on the whole provide a security for most of the group: a group moral neutrality will destroy the cohesion of the group because in a short time it will lack the binding force of loyalty to common ideals.

This is the most worrying thing about television. It exemplifies the twin principles of 'impartial' observation and free enterprise. (I put the word impartial in inverted commas because every observer evaluates what he sees and reports, his selection and presentation of the material is shaped by his own beliefs and prejudices.) It gives us a wide and valuable service of a very high technical standard. It opens for us all many delights of music, sport, entertainment, news, current affairs, and the natural world that previous generations have been denied. The people who are responsible for the content of our programmes take a pride in giving us the best service they can devise, but they also make it quite clear (through various annual reports, speeches and pamphlets) that their task is to reflect the values of society and not to shape them. This stance of objective observation and moral neutrality is unique in the history of civilisation. Each culture in the past has wanted to safeguard its ideals and its moral standards, whereas we encourage the open expression and practise of the widest varieties of moral choice. So the freedom to challenge and to break the traditional moral code, and to have your actions widely publicised and reported objectively helps to establish a new pattern of behaviour as the fashionable norm. People follow, not necessarily because they as individuals have weighed up the pros and cons and decided these are right, but more often because it seems to be the thing to do. An abdication of moral responsibility in what you portray for a mass audience inevitably influences the community to lose its respect for what now becomes unfashionable.

So, for example, in recent years television, radio and the press have frequently made great emphasis of people who have ignored the traditional moral principle that sexual relationships be confined to husband and wife within marriage. Some people had always broken the principle, but now it has become quite a feature to publicise those who do, as the adventurous, the daring, the amorous, the liberated ones. The publicity in fact does not just observe what is happening, but glamorises those who kick over the traces. Now we find the pressure to conform to the new morality pushes many reluctant young people to sexual relationships otherwise they are 'odd' or 'square', and produced the figures I saw a year or so ago that venereal disease is the second most common disease in this country after measles. Not all young people want early sexual experience, but many are pressurised into it to conform to the new code of behaviour.

Watching television is the national hobby, and most children watch a tremendous amount of it. It has inevitably a big influence in shaping their values, and if it is run by people who specifically disclaim any responsibility for shaping the values of society, what moral principles are we as a society training our younger generation in? It seems we are training them in the values of materialism and of entertainment, and indifference to any moral norms.

It is impossible to opt out of expressing through television in particular, moral principles which influence the whole of society, for every one of us is influenced by fashionable ideas. Freedom must go hand in hand with responsibility. We have the freedom to destroy our cultural, social and moral norms by the policy of declaring there are no norms except what is specifically against the law. We have to restrict our freedom if we are to do the responsible thing and decide there are certain moral values which are essential to the stability and security of the majority of people which we will emphasise again and again in our popular culture, and which we will not allow to be publicly ridiculed, nor will we give publicity to those who want to undermine those values.

Yet in popular culture at present we are often encouraged to laugh at dishonesty, tricks, lies and unfair behaviour. In the past, our humour could feature these things because the wholesome norms of behaviour—honesty, fairness, truth and kindness—were instilled into us in our formative years at home, at school, at church and in the neighbourhood. Now that these are no longer emphasised in the same way, we cannot afford to concentrate so much of our humour

25

and popular culture on deriding them. Similarly we cannot afford, for the sake of our norms of behaviour to feature death, violence, robbery and intimidation as often as we do.

The present cultural diet on television is defended on the grounds that many of the drama programmes which portray anti-social behaviour always end up with the good guys winning. In any case it is merely something for relaxation and entertainment and there is no evidence that it changes people's behaviour. Even if you accept that (which I do not) then on grounds of taste alone, is it not unseemly for a cultured and civilised people to spend a great deal of time being entertained by portrayals of the crudest and cruellest forms of human behaviour?

Every popular culture in history has not merely reflected the values of society, but moulded them too. Every popular culture in history has accepted that there are spiritual ideals and moral imperatives which it is the duty of society's leaders to emphasise, and the duty of parents to teach their children. Only decaying cultures have been reluctant to make moral choices in many fields of public and private behaviour, and have put the strongest emphasis on material benefits and individual rights, rather than on obligations of moral duty and public responsibility.

Material benefits are important and valuable. Our error has been to regard material comforts as the whole yardstick of progress. We have neglected to accord spiritual, emotional and social criteria equal importance.

The delicate balance of nature has taught us to be a great deal more humble in our use of the world. We have come to realise that drawing people away from the material poverty of the countryside, which nevertheless had for most people great emotional, cultural and spiritual richness, has brought to some material riches but spiritual impoverishment, and for the vast majority of people simply an exchange from one form of poverty and enslavement to another.

26

We do need to reassess what life is for, and how we live it. We need to understand our own basic physical, mental, spiritual and emotional needs. We need to reassess our responsibility to God, to each other, to ourselves, to the nation and the world, and to future generations.

To some extent this reassessment is going on nationally and internationally by politicians, experts, and people who shape public opinion. As part of this task, we, the ordinary folk in ordinary neighbourhoods, villages and towns can play our part. This book does not try to cover all the issues we could or should look at. Different groups will hopefully respond with interest and action on one or two of these and some groups will pursue issues not mentioned here.

The time for aimless and fruitless discussion is over. We must intend to act to shape the society we want in our own local area. We must also adopt a large dose of humility in our aims, for arrogance in the past and present has clearly done some good and great harm.

3

EDUCATION AND FAMILY LIFE

WE have reached the point where we must thoroughly re-examine the values and philosophy which will guide our actions and ideals in the future. We must decide what sort of society we do want. Far from just accepting what we already have and trying one or two little improvements, we need to move in a very different direction. To do so, we are forced back to the basis of ours and any culture or religion.

The Roman empire fell, and in the fall and the rebuilding of a new civilisation the Christian religion played a decisive role. The major force for reshaping our business civilisation will be a fresh presentation and expression of religious insights, challenging the current norms of behaviour, taking us forward to a different understanding of the meaning of life, and shaping our social organisation and activity to explore and celebrate that philosophy.

Such a redirection of our society will come from forces within and outside the traditional church organisation, by groups of dedicated people challenging the values and life-style of the moment by the way we live, the ideals and values we teach our children, and by the things we say.

In his book *Business Civilisation in Decline* (Marion Boyars, Publishers) quoted in *The Observer Review* 28 December 1975, Robert L. Heilbroner the economist forecasts the decline of what he calls the 'business civilisation' and the role that a new religion will have to play in building a new civilisation. He writes: 'A crucial element in the transformation of the Roman system into the wholly different medieval period was the influence of the new religion of Christianity which at first undermined the old order and later provided the spirit and shaped the institutional forms of the new order. So, too, in our future, I suspect that a major force for the transformation of business civilisation will be a new religious orientation, directed against the canons and precepts of our time, and oriented towards a wholly different conception of the meaning of life and a mode of social organisation congenial to the encouragement of that life.'

'What sort of religious orientation might this be? From our prior argument a high degree of political authority will be inescapable in the period of extreme contingency we can expect a hundred years hence. This augurs for the cultivation of nationalist, authoritarian attitudes, perhaps today foreshadowed by the kind of religious politicism we find in China. The deification of the State, whatever we may think of it from the standpoint of our still-cherished philosophies, seems therefore the most likely replacement for the deification of materialism that is the unacknowledged religion of our business culture.'

That does not follow. Religion is the most powerful force for good that shapes individual and community behaviour, and human beings need to be in communion with the Divine Power in life we call God. The summit of our understanding about true and abiding values, the noblest human behaviour, and the most mature understanding of human destiny is given to us by Jesus Christ. We have got into a rut in our thinking, and the forms of expressing Christian life and worship, and there is a lack of conviction among many Christians about the truth of Christian faith. We are searching for a new spiritual security.

We need to urge men and women today to look again at the Christian understanding of life and its purpose, and apply those insights in work, life-style, and our efforts to transform our society. It is of paramount importance that we are in the closest possible harmony with God's purpose for his creation.

In a perfect world we would see our children growing up happy, healthy, well-balanced, learning skills of mind and hand, fully enjoying family life, friendships, the world around us, the fulfilment of beauty in music, art, literature, enriching their lives by learning, and by a variety of experiences. But we all know only too well that we who are parents are not perfect, neither are our children or their teachers, or the influences other people have on them.

Life is lived by imperfect people, and this fact is pressed home upon us in every avenue of life. Other people's imperfections, weaknesses, irresponsibility, and awkwardness of temperament (and the results of our own) give to our life thousands of cuts great and small which hurt, wound, disappoint or upset us. We have to help our children to chart a course through life, a life that is not easy and in which some of their sufferings will be because of our actions.

What is the purpose of education? Is it to stimulate creative activity? Is it to impart basic skills of reading, writing, arithmetic? Is it to develop and train the character? Is it to widen individual horizons? Is it to develop physical and artistic gifts? Should it include the widest possible range of choice? How should the teaching be given? Many people dispute about the different styles of teaching available these days, ranging from the formal disciplined style that was traditional up to the late 1950s in most English schools to the informal self-exploratory style which has been tried more and more since the 1960s.

These questions are of fundamental importance to the well-being of our children. Most of us parents are too content to leave the style of teaching and the philosophy of life taught, to the professional teachers. This is due to a mixture of respect for the integrity and competence of the teaching profession, a preoccupation with our own jobs and other interests, and a diffidence about ruffling the feathers of those who teach our children. Parents, teachers and others need to explore together many matters of policy and principle which can affect the lives of our children permanently. For our children's sakes we ought not to let the philosophy of life we teach in schools become something we just accept. The whole basis of society rests on what we believe life is for, and this ought now to become the great national debate.

EDUCATION GROUPS

1. *In many neighbourhoods, parents or teachers (whether there is a formal Parent Teacher Association or not) could meet together for a limited time, say six meetings, in small groups of not more than twelve people in each group, to discuss the content and method of teaching in their schools, and the relationship between home and school. Here Christian parents and teachers can play an important role that requires sensitivity, a willingness to listen and learn from other people, and genuine humility.*

The purpose of such meetings is in the first place to have a full exchange of opinions, hopes and fears about our children and their education. Let us acknowledge that because of our church training we are too often inclined to view every issue from the point of view that if all the teachers, parents and children went to church regularly our problems of education and behaviour would be solved. This, we must acknowledge, is not true. The Church is a gathering of sinners just as much as any other gathering. The difference in theory is that the congregation is a gathering of sinners seeking forgiveness, grace, renewal and fellowship to grow in holiness, but human nature being what it is we can too easily consider ourselves rather arrogantly as those who are doing the right and proper thing, and inclined to tut-tut at those who do not join us. Arrogance and evangelism have no part in such group meetings as I envisage, but we need to prepare prayerfully and with self-discipline for such meetings if we

Christians are to permeate them with Christian insights.

In the exchange of opinions, which will at first be prickly and sensitive, both teachers and parents will be inclined to think that other people are criticising them personally. The Christian insight is to gently encourage people to speak the truth (as they see it) in love, to learn the difficult process of trusting each other and resisting the tendency to take entrenched positions and turn the whole exercise into a battle of words. If we can do this, then for all the imperfections on both sides, we and our children will all benefit.

Through growing in mutual trust, the group can move on to explore the purpose of education, and the right balance between basic skills, character development, creative activity, personal relationships and discipline.

As parents acknowledge and explain the difficulties of their role, and teachers do the same for theirs, so a common bond can be forged (even among people of quite different temperament and convictions) of mutual respect and sympathy. There will be many areas in which the group come to a common mind, and this may indicate changes being made both at home and at school in relationships with children. We shall soon see the need to work together in making these changes, perhaps to help our children and other people see the point of them, and we shall need both determination and a sense of humour to move in new directions.

One factor in this stage of the discussions will clearly need to be our understanding of human spirituality. Human beings are more than just a body and mind; the spirit, the soul, the character, call it what you will is that element within us that is creative, emotional, and reaches out with imagination to explore the heights and depths of human experience of love and suffering, of joy and sadness, and the complexity of life in poetry and prayer, in drama and prose, in music and art. The Christian experience is that the source of the human spirit is that Divine Spirit, the Person who created all that is, whom we call God. How our children are helped to perceive, experience and relate to God is clearly of the greatest importance in their development, and cannot be shrugged off either 'for' or 'against' God with pious or impious platitudes.

This is an area of life we are inclined to neglect, and people who have never been helped to reach out in loving trust to God are deprived of a relationship for which human beings are intended and in which we can find the paths of stability, fulfilment, forgiveness, love and joy (among others) in our journey through life. In his book *The Biology of God* (A scientist's study of man the religious animal) published by Jonathan Cape 1975. £4.50—the eminent Zoologist Sir Alister Hardy quotes Aldous Huxley (p. 4) 'Much of the restlessness and uncertainty so characteristic of our time is probably due to the chronic sense of unappeased desires from which men naturally religious, but condemned by circumstances to have no religion, are bound to suffer.' Religion is clearly an important matter in the education of our children.

SECONDARY EDUCATION
The purpose of education inevitably brings us to look at whether the secondary school curriculum should be geared to passing examinations, to early specialisation, or to a greater degree of general education. Are we aiming to turn out of our schools cultured and balanced youngsters with a wide range of interests, or do we force them into a system leading to further education strictly geared to the sort of career they think they might like to pursue? What many parents do not seem to realise is that these questions are frequently discussed by teachers and others in the educational profession, and if we parents show no genuine interest (and a desire to understand the problems the teachers face) then crucial decisions affecting the lives of our children can be taken without consulting us. Many teachers fear that consulting

33

parents will involve harangues and arguments, or that most parents are really not interested. So here is an important task in the local community for Christian parents and/or teachers to take up, the formation for a limited period of what are often called 'Frontier' groups in which people on two sides of a frontier—parents and teachers—meet to understand each other, to break down the isolation barrier of that frontier, learn from each other, share with each other, and learn then in what ways they can profitably help and support each other in the future.

Such groups can perhaps meet for a limited period each year, fresh groupings of people being formed each time. The purpose is not to look at the narrow field labelled 'religious education', but the wider field of education as such. It may be that there is strong suspicion among teachers if parents make the first approach about forming such groups (or the other way round if teachers make the first move) that the purpose is to try and 'sell' religion in schools. This suspicion is a sad reflection on the rather arrogant behaviour of some Christians (past and present), and therefore it will be wise to avoid the subject of religion in the early days of such groups until there is established an element of mutual trust and respect, friendship and freedom from bigotry by both sides.

RELIGION AND SCHOOL
However, at some stage it will be necessary to discuss religious education in the strict sense, because it deals with central issues of belief on what life is all about. Furthermore, current pressures are strong to end the dominant role of Christian faith in religious education in our state schools, and place it as one among many religious and political ideologies. Here, we Christians need to examine the pros and cons with the utmost care, for it may not be the wisest course to jump in with both feet and defend the teaching of Christianity as *the* English religion. Clearly the underlying values of our society now are not Christian, and

in the past twenty years we have seen a great deal of religious education done very half-heartedly by teachers who had lost, or were in process of losing, their Christian faith, and so used the opportunity to share with their pupils their own scepticism. There have been, and still are, very many teachers of Christian conviction, and many teachers who have with integrity taught religious beliefs they did not share, but if we seek to maintain the primacy of Christianity in schools, both in the worship and the teaching, we may run the risk of continuing to innoculate children against religious belief when they are taught about Christianity by those who do not share the faith.

If, on the other hand, churches and parents realise that the Christian faith will not be taught to children in state schools as a religion they are encouraged to believe and practise, then the responsibility will be thrown back on the parents and the churches to give Christian children this training. This could possibly be an important development leading to a much stronger sense of opting in to Christianity (rather than opting out), and a much more conscious commitment by whole families to Christian teaching and practise at home and at church. One of the difficulties about Christian evangelism in Britain nowadays is that everyone tends to think of themselves as Christian, and to reckon it makes no difference to your attitudes and behaviour at work or at home whether you belong to a church or not.

The hardest thing for Christianity to battle against is not opposition and disagreement, but indifference. The pressure to end the dominant role of Christianity in religious education in our state schools sounds honourable enough in theory: 'because most people are not practising church members the state has no responsibility to teach what only a minority seem to believe. Give the children the widest possible choice of religious knowledge and let them opt themselves for the one they prefer.' That sounds very democratic, but it can also be an abdication of responsibility. Too wide a choice can sometimes paralyse our decision-making.

Every civilised society needs to pass on to its rising generation the highest, the noblest, the truest that it knows. No civilisation can afford to start afresh with every generation on choice of moral values, laws, beliefs, and ideals either in religion or in political theory, geometry, or physical science. We inherit the experience, the culture and the wisdom of our fore-fathers who have tested theories in their own lives, and passed on that which they found to be true. We can test and discover its truth for ourselves. We can do this in religion as well as in science. At this moment, scientific humanism which in its heyday was thought to have debunked Christianity is now found wanting as the answer to our social, cultural and political needs precisely because of its spiritual poverty.

It may be that opinion at the present time will oust Christianity from its dominant place in our state education system, if so this will give to Christians a powerful platform on which to campaign for parents to accept the responsibility of teaching our own children the Christian faith. This should help to strengthen the bonds in family life, and develop a spirit of joyful religious celebration in our homes.

BELIEVER'S BAPTISM

If Christianity becomes one part of the religious education syllabus in state schools among a study of Hinduism, Bhuddism, Mohammedanism, Humanism and perhaps too Marxism and other ideologies, then it will certainly be time to call in question our tradition of baptising babies. In the past, the common assumptions of society were Christian, and the teaching given in schools was Christian too. The influences a child received at home, in the neighbourhood, at church and at school all supported each other in teaching Christian faith, and upholding Christian ideals. That is no longer so, and if Christianity is no longer taught in schools as a religion they are encouraged to believe and practise, then it will be indefensible for the churches to try and maintain a system suitable for a secure, stable and Christian community life in our mobile and pluralistic society.

Already most parents have no intention of giving a baptised child training in Christian faith and life either at home or at church, but children grow up knowing they have been baptised, the parents feel they have done their religious duty to the child, and if the child wants to opt out then that is his choice. We parents have a responsibility to share our religious insights and convictions, our values and ideals with our children, and to encourage them to come to their own commitment to Christ. Having the child baptised, and doing next to nothing more about it, is to seriously neglect the spiritual and religious development of the child.

I was baptised at seventeen by my own choice, and the significance of the sacrament meant a great deal to me at the time. I now regret having had my own children baptised as babies, because I have denied to them the great experience of the personal commitment to Christ, the sacramental washing away of sin, and the new birth in Christian life. It seems to me now that in the ecumenical contacts, we have much to learn from the Baptist churches. Perhaps just as in the last hundred years our Church of England and the Free Churches have come to 'rediscover' the eucharist as the central act of Christian worship, so renewal in mission and unity, personal commitment, and Christian education and family religious training may depend upon us 'rediscovering' baptism in its original and evangelistic context of adult preparation of catechumens. Baptism ought to be the consequence of an encounter with the Gospel, not a preliminary to such an encounter. Christian membership ought to be something people opt into, and not out of.

The significance of the baptismal service, of the symbolic death and resurrection, the commitment, and the personal understanding and experience of what

Christ's death and resurrection means to every Christian, is more powerfully conveyed by adult baptism than anything else.

CHRISTIAN CONFIDENCE

If Christians in the future, living in a basically non-Christian environment, are to discover confidence in understanding, believing and practising their faith, then I believe the Christian community must become a self-conscious community of believers, rather than an amorphous mass of people who are technically Christians because they were baptised at the same age as they were vaccinated and it means as little to them.

We do not deprive children of anything by not baptising them. We do not cut them off from God's love, nor from the hope of eternal life. On the other hand, by baptising them before they are able to choose for themselves, we deprive them of the joy of making that choice, and deprive them of the deeply satisfying and enriching experience of turning to Christ as their own discovery, and of entering into Christian membership by their own choice.

Sir Alister Hardy in the book I mentioned earlier in this chapter, *The Biology of God*, writes, 'The reason why so many people doubt that science can in any way be concerned with religion is that they have come to accept an idea which is nothing more than a dogma: the supposition that everything that is truly scientific must eventually be reduced to physical and chemical terms. This is methodologically false' (p. 18). In beginning to explore religious experience scientifically he quotes with approval the point made by Edwin Starbuck in 1902, 'Science has conquered one field after another, until now it is entering the most complex, the most inaccessible, and of all, the most sacred domain—that of religion.... The study of religion is today where astronomy and chemistry were four centuries ago' (p. 21).

He writes at the end of his book, 'Religion is not

rational, it is essentially emotional. If it is to be real and to work, it must be as deep and sincere as human love. Without such sincerity, or emotion, faith if you like, it makes no response at all; with the right approach, however, lives can be transformed, seemingly impossible tasks achieved, and the drabness of the world turned into joy. Religion is at the heart of civilization' (p. 232). His is a scientist's way of putting it, but clearly, however we describe religious experience, this is something deep and central to human life that we have a responsibility to help our children experience and enter into so that they can know how to depend upon and trust the powerful Personal spiritual power we know as God our Father, and to walk with him through the difficulties of life.

This is the basic point behind the plea to re-examine in these days our inherited practice of baptising infants. We must provide the best possible way of helping children and young people to explore for themselves the mysteries of life and faith, to enter into a powerful religious experience that can lead them to a solid and secure spiritual foundation and relationship for life, and illumine their hopes and longings with faith and love.

2. Some groups of people who feel concerned about this can gather together and explore the pros and cons of the situation, trying as they do to look sensitively at our present baptismal practice, and to learn from the teaching of the Baptist Christians by inviting at least two of them to join each group. There is the Biblical practice to be examined, and local clergy can suggest or lend books to help the groups look at the whole question intelligently.

The exercise is concerned to explore a traditional practice of the Church which was developed in very different times to our own, and to see if this is really still the best normal practice for the Church to maintain. It is a search for what is right, and for what is truly best for the religious experience and growth for

future generations. Most of our religious practices have changed over the centuries; what we do now is something previous generations of Christians may have resisted with some spirit when it was introduced, or reintroduced, after a gap of many centuries. Our concern is much more for what seems to be right, rather than either changing for the sake of change, or refusing to change for no other reason than 'we've never done it that way'.

3. *We need to develop Christian family practices, starting when children are very tiny, that link home with church at the festival times and in the simple dramas of joy or of self-discipline give to our children a framework of festivals they can carry with them throughout their lives which help them to relate the hopes, fears and joys of human relationships to their faith and their life with God.*

In their formative years we give to our children a host of experiences which become memories, which help them to enjoy the richness, the wonder, the drama of life, and helps them to form values, ideals of behaviour, which they try to apply in both the loving and the hurtful experiences of their lives. Most adults recollect from childhood so many delightful experiences that are nostalgic and formative; almost all of them are simple family rituals they so enjoyed like putting the Christmas decorations up, mother's goodnight kiss, tea by the fire or roasting chestnuts in the garden every October. We shall deprive our children of so many rich experiences if we allow the pressures and strains of life to push out these regular shared family experiences.

Christmas
The obvious ritual for nearly every family with young children is Christmas Eve and the preparation for Father Christmas coming. We Christians have allowed

40

It is in many such ways as these, observing the Christian festivals in our homes as well as in church that we can share together the joys and the sorrows of Christ's life. They provide natural points within family life to discuss together matters of life and death, of suffering and sacrifice, of courage and willpower, celebration, joy and hope, of grace and inner strength, of wonder and mystery and awe, of prayer and of praise. Keeping the festivals enriches our life, and gives us all spiritual and emotional anchors in our faith and in each other, which will enable us to realise more clearly how we can relate our faith to the issues we face in daily life, and so help us create the sort of society we want.

4

WORK AND
RELATIONSHIPS

OUR religious activities at home or at church are the
means by which we celebrate and renew our vision
of what life is for. We are human beings and in us
there is something of the Divine life. The scientist has
not fully explained human life just by describing our
physical and chemical properties: energy and mind
are different but related elements in our human make-
up. So whatever our activity we must be concerned
to foster the human qualities, and struggle always to
organise our relationships at work to prevent people
being treated simply as units of production. Every
human being is unique, and is of special and particular
importance to God our Creator.

We are all sinners, and any hopes of creating the
sort of society we would ideally like to have, has to
recognise the strength and depth of sin in every human
being. We are born like this, and by our own choice
we can exaggerate the harmful effects to ourselves and
other people of that sin by feeding it and allowing
it in so many ways to rule our life and mar our happiness. Sin is not just personal selfishness (that is only
part of it) but includes our insensitivity to other
people, their feelings, their working conditions, their
hopes. It includes injustice, organising things so that
while certain people may prosper others will suffer. It
includes that closed-mind attitude which will not or
cannot see another point of view. It includes exploiting
other people, treating them as less than fellow children
of God.

The word salvation, which Christians often use,
means healing, like the ointment (salve) which soothes

44

and helps to make whole again where now there is a painful wound. The words 'health', 'healing', 'wholeness' all come from the same Old English word as 'holiness'.

The Christian concern for salvation should not in the first place be to develop a religiosity in people, but to bring the spirit of healing and wholeness to the everyday affairs of men and women. Christ bids us show care, compassion and courage (like the Good Samaritan, Luke 10.29–37), learn the difficult skill of forgiving and making new each time there is a damaged relationship, a misunderstanding, or a hurt between us and another person or persons (Matthew 18.21–35). Through the way we live we demonstrate our faith. We shall certainly also seek to share our convictions with those who want to know, for there is no more delightful experience for a Christian than helping another person to come to his own knowledge of and commitment to Christ. However, our vocation as Christians at work is not to bait a sprat to catch a mackerel but to bring the spirit of healing, reconciliation, justice and peace to work.

In doing so we follow in the traditions of the prophets of the Scriptures like Amos, a hill-farmer who felt impelled to speak out against the injustice he could see—'they sell the needy for a pair of shoes' (Amos 2.6) and calls on his people to 'Hate evil, and love good, and establish justice' (5.6). Those like Jeremiah and Hosea had to suffer as they did their duty in calling society to seek better values, a truer justice, and try to create the sort of society and people for which God has created us. St Paul too worked long and hard at the difficult business of mending quarrels, building new relationships, urging better conduct. Jesus Christ himself came with the word of healing and an invitation to human beings to enter into a new and fuller relationship with God and with each other: for this he was crucified. It is not easy, but it is right. Let us now look at one or two ways in which we can try to relate our faith to our work.

Whatever job we do, the heart of it is still how we get on with other people, and how other people treat us. Relationships at work are harmed by a foreman unfairly picking on a worker he doesn't like, or the suspicion between workers who are classed as 'non-skilled' or 'semi-skilled' (yet because of years of experience their knowledge and ability has become a skill in itself) and those in the craft unions who have had to serve apprenticeships. An almighty row can blow up when a worker is accused of slacking, and it is difficult to know whether he is or has been unable to work because a manager has failed to organise properly the flow of materials to him to enable him to work. New ways of working are introduced, and the biggest problem that causes rows, bad feelings, and sour relationships may not be the new method or the different way of paying for the job, but the way the idea was introduced, the lack of consultation or proper explanation.

So much of good relationships at home or at work rests upon our view of human beings as individual people who have an innate dignity because everyone is a child of God, and we each have a hidden inner nature which is sensitive, easily hurt. In trying to create understanding, in trying to ask questions like 'Is this right?' 'Is this fair?' 'Are you being fair to the other person's point of view?' 'Are you assuming that because the other person seems more posh, or on the other hand more shy and less able to explain what they feel than you are, that they are less human than you?' you will inevitably be criticised by your own colleagues as well as others.

If you try to raise deeper questions about a firm's responsibility not only to its shareholders, employees, retired workers and customers, but also to the community at large, the environment, and further afield to the producers of its raw materials, perhaps in poor countries, you will be touching sensitive points. But all these are very important areas of conflict at work.

To say or do nothing may be to support things that are not fair or right. Often it will not be easy to see what is the right thing to do, for in our complicated industrial society a change of practice may have repercussions on many other people. To stop a process that is dangerous to your workers, or to the local environment, may put many other people out of work.

We live in a society in which it is more and more difficult to see moral issues in terms of black and white —instead they appear to be many different shades of grey, and to choose the 'right' thing to do, may be to choose merely the lesser of two evils. But because we believe that we should seek in life the truest flowering of the human spirit and character, and for this we should constantly seek to heal the wounds that damage or make sick our humanity, we have to be healing agents at work as well as in the other spheres of life. Healing may in some cases be a soothing of troubled relationships, but in others a painful cut may be needed to drain away a poison.

CHRISTIAN GROUPS
4. *If Christians are to play their full part in this godly calling, to be sometimes reconcilers, sometimes prophets we need to find a spiritual anchor with other Christians of prayer, reflection, support and encouragement. A small group of Christians who meet regularly at home, or in the lunch-hour, or at a pub, sports centre, pigeon loft, or on the train to and from work can provide for each other that important support group. In such a group they can share the frustrations, the hopes, the problems of their work and relate them to the calling of God to be faithful to the vision of human life and activity we see in Jesus Christ.*

We can draw great strength from such a group, strength that will enable us to cope with the heavy and conflicting demands at work, and enable us to reflect on the meaning of our work. Is work just a boring, exhausting activity we do to earn money? Should we seek to create in the way the work is organised, opportunity for variety, creativity, and better human relationships so that it is possible to find satisfaction in the work itself, as well as in what the wages provide and sustain?

The way work is organised, the philosophy of life on which the business is run, is not something we just have to endure, and thereby sentence our children's and grandchildren's generations to endure too, but something in which we seek to reflect the life of God, truly human values. It is important to remember too, that in the lives of every one of our workmates God is active, whether they recognise Him, believe in Him, worship Him, or not. We must seek to be in tune with His purpose, to understand more of what he wants us to express in our work, that activity which occupies us so much and upon which so much depends.

5. *To discuss particular problems it is important to gather together a group of people at work to include both sides of any 'frontier', and to include both Christians and non-Christians. The group is invited to meet together six times, and the problem discussed. The purpose is not just a talking shop, aimless chatter, but to develop bridges of understanding between both sides, and to move towards areas of common agreement.*

Into such discussions can come, in an honest exchange of opinion, insights from theology about the meaning and purpose of life. For some man, hounded, ridiculed, 'sent to Coventry', to see his experience as a crucifixion may greatly help him to bear the pain and look forward to a new glory, and to see that every experience no matter how apparently futile or purposeless has its place in our human development, and that great souls are those who have come through suffering.

In the puzzled groping for a pattern with which we can make some sort of sense of a discussion about using raw materials, processing them and the effect

48

of this process on our local environment, the Christian understanding of Creation and man's responsibility to God as a steward for the earth which is entrusted to him, and our answerability to God for the way in which we use these things are important philosophical guidelines. Margaret Kane in her book *Theology in an Industrial Society* (S.C.M.) gives in detail how such groups can relate theology to work, and the role that Christian men and women can play in shaping the sort of industrial society we want.

POLITICS IN INDUSTRY

Some discussions are best organised outside the factory or office where we work, and rooted in the life of the local church as some of its members seek to help each other relate faith to life, and pursue the search for justice in work. Other discussions will crop up informally in the works canteen, or as a group of people discuss the urgent problem of the moment, or as managers chew over together their long-term plans, or management and union leaders explore together a problem in industrial relations.

Other matters can only be tackled within the 'political' structures of industry, in union branch meetings, trades council meetings, management and other professional institute meetings. Those Christians who recognise their vocation to take a full part in these meetings and to accept positions of authority and responsibility as shop stewards or branch officials will need a considerable sense of support from their fellow Christians. They may have to decide between attending a church service or meeting and attending a union or institute meeting. They may be a lone voice of concern for the underdog, or for reason and fairness, or to remind a committee meeting that the organisation exists for the welfare of all their members and not to support the chairman in his vendetta against one or two awkward members.

To be able to go back from this and relax in the company of fellow Christians who share the same

49

vision of what we are all trying to create in society can be an enormous source of strength to anyone. To face a difficult meeting or decision knowing that you can rely upon God, and the prayerful concern and support of your fellow Christians can brace many a fearful and nervous soul to meet challenges they would otherwise regard as impossible. Remember the story of David and Goliath, an example of godly strength in human weakness achieving what human strength alone could not defeat.

It may be that a band of men who call each other Brothers need to hear other opinions besides those of the most vocal leaders, and they may not want to. It may be right for a Christian to put a point of view he does not agree with, so that it is fully taken into account before a decision is made. He may need to witness to the moral rightness of sticking to an agreement freely entered into, and to speak out against deceit, stealing or lies. He may have to draw attention to dangers or drawbacks in new methods of work even though these may appear to harm the interests of his own group. He may have to take steps to discourage racialist attitudes at work, and encourage folk to value a person by their character and ability not by the colour of their skin or the accent of their voice.

These are all issues which face any Christian worker or manager. It all sounds like a tall order, as though work is a constant battleground, in which the Christian is called to daily crucifixion. Our Lord did tell us that 'If any man would come after me, let him deny himself and take up his cross and follow me. For whoever would save his life will lose it; and whoever loses his life for my sake and the gospel's will save it' (Mark 8.34–6).

However, we are not called to see life always as some grim battle, it is also to enjoy, to love and to be loved, to give and receive pleasure, to bind up the broken-hearted, preach liberty to the captives, give sight to the blind, and help the lame to walk. Christian life is a search for love, goodness, godliness in every human activity, and to do our utmost to pull down the barriers we all are inclined to build and fence ourselves into our narrow group and rigid pattern of thinking. There needs to be the mark of genuine joy on the face of the Christian at work, who battles for goodness and justice when necessary not because he loves a fight but because he loves. The spirit we seek is not a dour Puritan kill-joy search for righteousness, but a gay and a courageous search for all men and women to have what Jesus came to bring, 'I came that they might have life, and have it abundantly' (John 10.10). It springs from the calling of God to care, to serve, to help, to do your best for other people whether they appreciate this or not and whether they recognise their God or not. The power to live in this way comes only from putting down spiritual roots into the Scriptures, into prayer, and into the supportive fellowship of other Christians.

SOME KEY PROBLEMS AT WORK

Discussing problems of work with a group of men in my own parish—we met monthly in an upstairs room of a local pub—we have concluded after several meetings that there are four key areas of concern today. These are:

1. Size and responsibility in organisations.
2. Moral values at work.
3. Our work, our money, and our freedom to spend it as we wish.
4. Motivation and discipline.

The members of our group were drawn from a wide range of jobs and firms, and too from a wide range of responsibility from the shop floor to senior management. It included people in local government, education and professional partnerships, as well as retired people. Together we were trying to explore in what ways we Christians can influence directly our own firm, council, school, profession or community towards the sort of society we want.

Size and responsibility in organisations

People who work in large firms like I.C.I. or British Steel, are not the only ones who are deeply concerned that organisations have grown beyond comfortable human dimensions. Similar concerns have come up with the organisation of government social services, with education, and with the complicated laws which now regulate such a wide section of human affairs. In large organisations decisions can get lost in the maze of consultations, or a decision by one plant within the group may be stymied by the veto of another. Mountains of forms feed the demands of central organisers. The whole process can breed various new forms of inefficiency and bad management: a shop steward who knows his plant manager cannot make a certain decision finds it more satisfactory to go over his head, leaving the front-line manager frustrated and dissatisfied.

For the sake of human well-being we must question the doctrine that bigger is better, and discourage rationalisation for the sake of rationalisation. There are many people in local government who are deeply unhappy about the reorganisation that took place when the new County and District Councils were created. It seems to be true that the bigger the organisation, the less each individual within it counts. It was thought to be more cost-effective, but many voices are now being raised in industry, commerce and government to question whether this is always so. One small example that comes to mind here is the improvement in staff morale and customer service in a hotel that formerly belonged to British Rail, and in which all decisions had to be vetted by Head Office, to the situation now that it has been bought by a couple of local businessmen who take a close and personal interest in it.

Local decision-making can be imaginative and flexible: central decision-making can be cumbersome, time-wasting and unimaginative. Money is often wasted, and staff less conscientious when final responsibility is not to the local manager or owner, but to a remote Board or Chief Executive. Lord Mountbatten notes in his autobiography that Pandit Nehru told him he would succeed in his relationships with Indian leaders seeking independence because he had plenipotentiary powers. All previous Viceroys had to refer key decisions back to London, but Lord Mountbatten was able to make his decisions himself, put them into action and then report back.

It is becoming more important to organise work and other activities to as small units as possible, allowing the maximum freedom in local decision-making. In our church life too we need to value the contribution Congregationalist thinking can bring to ecumenical discussions and not allow that distinctive witness to be lost in a sea of Synods. The words of the former Archbishop of Canterbury Michael Ramsey are appropriate here: 'Revolutionary movements in the Church have commonly happened not by a collective decision that it would be a good thing for such and such to be done, but by someone making a start and others following.'

THE MAGIC PORRIDGE POT

Historians of the future may well find that our current interest in devolution is related to the increasing centralisation and bureaucracy, together with the growth in the number of our activities that are regulated by laws. The whole situation is rather like the overflowing Magic Porridge Pot in the children's story book which engulfed everyone and everywhere in the sticky, cloying super-abundance of goodness that went way beyond its original purpose. People were trapped in what was intended to merely help and sustain them, and give them a better life.

Can we accept, and persuade other people to accept inconsistency? If we can let decision-making rest more and more in the local community, the local plant, we will find that what happens in one place does not happen in another. This may make some people

53

envious, or cross because they think it is ridiculous, but there is no reason why every community from Land's End to John o' Groats should all adopt the same priorities and methods of working for the sake of national policy.

6. *The truly human community is not one that is identical to every other, but the one in which you can know and be known, and in which by your efforts you can change policy and improve the local lot. It is important to press this point in works discussions, in local policy-making bodies, to your M.P., through the local branch of your political party, through the local newspaper, through neighbourhood action groups, school managers, Parent Teacher Associations, Parish Councils, and local branches of unions, managerial bodies and other things you belong to in your own area. The trend to centralisation stems not from some inevitable and unstoppable law of progress but from a current fashion of thought. Fashions can change and we can help change them.*

Moral values at work
The cost in cash terms of sin at work is enormous. Every firm pays great sums to insure against theft, arson and negligence. Security systems, crime prevention and auditing costs are high. The loss every year in pilfering runs into many many millions of pounds. Simply because we cannot trust everyone to be honest and conscientious we add a staggering burden to the balance sheet of every organisation and firm.

The crisis of trust in business today appears to be growing. People in a wide range of business activities tell me that it is increasingly difficult to rely upon a promise given or a statement made. For example, one of our group in charge of a building site ordered a roller to be delivered for a demonstration at 10 a.m. the following day. It did not arrive. On the telephone he was told it had been dispatched at 8.30 a.m., although he later discovered it had not been dispatched until after the phone call, and the person he was talking to knew that it hadn't. This is just one of so many examples of the breakdown in trust that appears to be growing.

Similarly there is a developing problem of conscientiousness. There are many examples of people skiving, and doing it regularly. These examples come from all levels of responsibility. It is not just the two council employees I see often making use of quiet side streets week after week to waste half an hour or so, but it applies too to managers with extra long lunch hours. One man I have to deal with for parish matters quite often I know is never available between 12 noon and 2 p.m.

SIN IS EXPENSIVE

Plain and simple sin is costing our country a lot of money. You do not stop it by passing laws against it, nor by punishing hard the offenders who get caught. You may contain it and restrict it by these means but the roots of sin lie in the human heart. If boosting production and efficiency is what we want to do, then it is the inner man and woman we have to change. It is simply not true to say that you cannot change human nature: the Christian experience is precisely the opposite. An encounter with Christ can transform the ideals, the behaviour, the values and the actions of any person. We are still sinners, still far from perfect, but a spiritual encounter with the living God creates a new perspective in the soul, and channels our desires into wholesome paths. The call Jesus made when he began his teaching ministry rings down the centuries and still draws response in souls today: 'Repent and believe the Gospel' (Mark 1.15). The meaning of the word repent is to turn your life round, walk in a different direction, change your goals in life.

There may be many people we work with who have not the slightest desire to do that. We disagree with their values and ideals maybe, but we know too that trying to force Christ down their throats is very likely under normal conditions to make them resentful, angry, feel they are being 'got at' or threatened, or perhaps being subject to moral blackmail. But as we long for others to share our vision of what life could be, and work towards it, we must still raise the issues of honesty, integrity, trust, reliability and so on in our discussions at work.

7. *It is right and honest, from time to time to make it clear (and this may call for considerable courage from us) that the root of our own integrity and search for what is best in life lies in our religious faith. If we fail to do that, our witness is no more than giving the impression of good humanism. Human nature needs (Sir Alister Hardy believes this may be a biological need, a simple fact of our human make-up which it is folly to try and ignore) a relationship of child to parent with God. This is essential for us to grow in true humanity, and cut the powerful cords that draw us deeper and deeper into the moral mire of unredeemed humanity.*

There are an abundance of deep moral problems and spiritual malaise in our society today that have not been cured by increased prosperity, better education, improved medical services, or progressive legislation. As all these very desirable changes have taken place, yet new problems have arisen. The root of all these problems is in the minds, values and ambitions of people. Secularism cannot save us, for it does not aim to change human nature but to feed human desires. We are acutely aware of this in the workaday world, so it is clear that a responsibility rests on every Christian to point towards the human spirit as the root of our crisis of culture, national identity, and economic difficulties.

This is a matter of shifting public opinion. It is a task we cannot shrug off and say is the responsibility of bishops, politicians or newspaper leader-writers. A pearl in the oyster grows simply because a bit of grit gets into the system. Each one of us can feed in the grit that challenges whenever necessary the assumption that you cannot change human nature, or that laws and punishments, better wages or working conditions are all that is needed to make people good. Perhaps because so many folk do not like nowadays to use the word 'good', and prefer instead phrases like 'socially responsible' we dress things up too much in unplain language that does not convey what we really mean. There are many discussions each one of us is involved in day by day, when the whole matter of behaviour, good and bad actions, are talked about. Let each one of us set to and make this point as often as possible until bit by bit it becomes the new fashion of thought: the medicine for our national sickness is honesty, integrity, trust, reliability, and justice: the spring in human hearts from whence they flow is faith and trust in God and a wholehearted response to the vision of life we have been shown in Jesus Christ.

Our work, our money, and our freedom to spend it as we wish
This is a considerable bone of contention with many workers these days. The benefits of the government, law, defence, police, education, medical and welfare services, planning, consumer protection and all the other government agencies have to be paid for. Because there are so many of them the bill is a big one, and it has reached the point where more than half a working wage can be taken in tax, whether directly through income tax and taxes like the road fund licence, or indirectly through V.A.T. and other means. On the one hand there are calls for a reduction in tax, but the moment this affects one of the services we have come to value like education or hospital care then there are howls of protest.

Here again we Christians need to do a straightforward information job again and again. It seems so obvious, plain common sense, but to many people it is something entirely new and surprising that getting the state to do everything for us in the way things are now done arises from the current fashion of thought and may not be the best (or most economic!) way of dealing with our problems. Many millions of pounds are spent on National Health Service facilities and prescriptions, and all doctors are trained in hospital methods to remove diseases, yet they are overworked not with treating natural diseases but in responding to illnesses which are emotional in origin and rise from damaged relationships in the family and the society of the patients. A great deal of illness is caused by the things we do to ourselves, and the abuses of our bodies with drugs like nicotine, alcohol, tranquillisers, wrong diet, and the lack of appropriate physical, mental and spiritual exercises.

The financial cost of loneliness and unhappiness which make such demands upon welfare and medical services are a symptom of the bleak community life we have organised in so many new housing areas, or in separating old people from their children and grand-children.

WE SUFFER FROM SPIRITUAL POVERTY
8. *The answer is to suggest society sets different priorities, and works towards different goals. Is it too harsh to suggest that we teach people the dangers of abusing the human body and then whoever chooses to ignore this cannot expect to be treated free of charge? They abuse the National Health Service, and endanger the quality of treatment available to those who have not habitually created their own sickness. Would it not save money, and reduce the pressure on the severely over-strained N.H.S. to shift more emphasis to health education?*

Offer both the carrot and the stick: health comes from healthy living and for most of us the solution is in our own hands throughout our life, so if we choose to ignore this we shall have to provide our own treatment when our folly catches up with us. We can reduce the demand for extra medical, police and welfare services by self-restraint, and positively trying to create truly human communities (and this town planners and architects can respond to) and moving towards the ideal of care for the weak and elderly resting again with the extended family unit and the local neighbourhood. It is a spiritual and social vision we need that pulls away from all human care being a professional service.

To some this plea may sound like old-fashioned Toryism, a mixture of 'God helps those who help themselves', 'Blow you Jack, I'm all right', 'Devil take the hindmost' and 'The weakest to the wall'. I am not seeking a philosophy of life that is harsh for the sake of being harsh, nor one that is unsympathetic to the very weak-willed and those who genuinely need help to cope with the difficult business of modern living particularly the very young, and the aged and infirm. But it is time to question whether the deep encroachment on everyone's freedom to earn money and choose how to spend most of what they earn has not arisen because by trying to cushion everyone from the results of their own folly or misadventure we have sapped the will of too many to stand on their own feet, to plan and provide for themselves and their own family, and to freely give (and enjoy giving) service in their own neighbourhood and community which is human, personal and enduring.

ACHIEVEMENTS OF A SMALL GROUP

It is human nature—unredeemed human nature that is—to abuse a service which we feel we have paid for, will cost us nothing at the point of use, and one we can demand as of right. State paternalism seems to me in these relatively affluent days to be not crediting us with the sense and maturity to budget for ourselves. More and more decisions are taken out of our own hands and in the long run this is almost certainly a deep threat to our personal freedom, and moral responsibility.

These are matters which are often discussed in chats at work, or can be raised when relevant matters are on the agenda of whatever local organisation we belong to. The whole subject could well be the subject for many 'Frontier' groups. It is important to remember that although it's a hackneyed phrase it is still true that 'great oaks from little acorns grow'. A discussion group of about half a dozen men in a vicarage study at Leamington Spa studying the Bible had their attention switched to 'What can we do about the plight of children suffering in Viet Nam?' during the war there. At the tea-break, the Vicar's wife explained her own distress as she had watched a report from Julian Pettifer on the news which featured children orphaned by the war. From the vision shared and worried over and prayed about in that small group of ordinary folk, members of an ordinary parish church, near neighbours with no special qualifications or any experience in international action, grew Project Viet Nam Orphans. It raised money to send nurses to care for orphans in Saigon, ran an orphanage eventually, and brought many children to this country for adoption. Whether or not you agree that it was wise to bring the children out of their own country is beside the point for the moment. I quote this example simply to show that no matter how small the group, in any ordinary neighbourhood it is possible for a vision to be shared and extraordinary things to be achieved from the discussion, prayer and the decision to act and not be put off by the overwhelming size of the problem. It is better to have done a little, than to have done nothing.

9. *One or two small groups of people can find that as they seek to do something constructive the Spirit of God can take hold of their small venture and create something substantial, and they achieve what they formally thought was impossible. The assumptions, goals, expectations of society today can be changed,*

and this can begin in the activities of one or two—or many—small groups.

Motivation and discipline

If work is organised so that it is intensely boring or unpleasant then there is not much encouragement to be conscientious about it. On the other hand if it is enjoyable, creative, fulfilling, then the pleasure of doing the job and doing it well is motivation enough for most folk. I know many people who would not change their job to a better paid one because they are happy doing the job they have.

If on the other hand it is repetitious work the main attraction is the pay. An individual on a bonus scheme, anxious to get the largest possible pay packet, is not likely to miss the bus to work, take days off without notice, or turn out work that is likely to be rejected (if rejects are paid less than work that is passed).

I hear from many people in very different types of work, reports that people are less conscientious, less loyal to the firm for which they work than people used to be. Some suggest that because few people deeply fear the sack, or because social security takes away the gravest anxieties about being unemployed, that there is less motivation and discipline because there is less fear of the consequences of unemployment.

Lectures on management principles emphasise the stock list of motivators, fear, pay, force, job satisfaction and so on. I have never heard it suggested that dedication to a concept, a philosophy of life, a religious faith, a deeply held conviction is a powerful motivator at work. Yet you realise from people in voluntary work that deeply held convictions can be very strong motivators. If we feel there is value to other people—people we feel responsible for or want to help—in the job we do, then this in itself creates a strong motive for doing the job and doing it well. There is all the difference in the world between a nurse who nurses primarily because she wants to care

61

for people in need and the nurse who nurses because she needs to earn money, and this is the job she has taken. More money does not increase the latter's conscientiousness. The motivator is in the nurse's philosophy of life.

It is a very grave mistake to neglect this too in industry. Just as a dedicated Maoist in a large industrial concern will be motivated not to get the best paid job, but to get the job that gives him the best opportunity to spread the gospel of Maoism, to exercise leadership and influence, so a determination to create the sort of society we want can motivate and discipline people with different philosophies of life. If you believe that your work, however tedious it is, has value in the purpose of God, and that you can do your part to further that purpose by the way you behave, you can make a significant contribution in any job to a more conscientious approach to work and the well-being of society.

10. *We Christians must emphasise whenever the subject of motivation comes up, that belief and trust in God, can be the most powerful motivator for conscientious work. Conscience (our sense of responsibility to God for what we say, think and do), is a far more powerful internal policeman to prevent irresponsible and anti-social behaviour than fearsome punishments.*

There are many jobs which provide their own motivation to work by the demands made upon you as you do them. A bus driver cannot choose to slack, for the demands of the time-table and the traffic provide a joint discipline which he cannot avoid. Nevertheless there are many tasks which provide us with the freedom to slack off if we choose, and there is no doubt that a worker who has an inner integrity and conscientiousness in doing his job is invaluable to the firm. This again is a spiritual quality arising from convictions about what life is for and how we should behave. Godliness is a very powerful motivator.

PREVENT AGGRAVATIONS

This whole subject of motivation and discipline is one we need to work on and look at from many angles, for certainly a firm can lose a great deal if many employees are not conscientious. The problem of discipline comes to the fore very often in industrial relations. An unofficial strike may occur simply because one or two influential people do not accept the disciplines of normal negotiating machinery, or the decision reached through that machinery. The public at large is often too quick to jump to the conclusion that the fault is entirely that of the workers, shop stewards or union officials who call the strike. It is on some occasions the fruit of insensitive and stupid stances taken by managers, or a breakdown in trust when management break a promise given. In such cases the indiscipline of a manager who cannot control his tongue, or who breaks his word is not pilloried in the Press in the same way as the strikers.

The Christian responsibility is clearly not fulfilled if we jump to rash conclusions when we have only heard one side of the story, or if we criticise as lazy and undisciplined people who may have been provoked over a long period to action which erupts in an unofficial strike. There are we know in some firms small groups of men and/or women determined to aggravate any small dispute for political ends. They can only get to work on a real or imagined grievance. It is part of our responsibility, at whatever level we work, to try and prevent such aggravations, and to urge a spirit of discipline on both sides for the long-term good of both employers and employees.

SABBATICAL LEAVE

Two further points are related to this problem of motivation and discipline. The trend these days is towards automation, providing one machine to replace many workers. Reduction of the work-force is one of management's objectives in so many firms, and some observers of the industrial scene in County Cleveland tell me that as a nation we shall have to accept a large number of people being unemployed. They suggest to me that this is going to be a permanent feature of the industrial scene in the future. If so, then in and out of work we must explore the implications of this for the well-being of working men and women (and redundancy when it comes no longer stops at the shop floor workers but reaches up to the highest grades of management too). Is the answer to reduce overtime and keep more people employed? Is it better to reduce the working week for everyone?

11. *Can we create sabbatical years of freedom for many workers to take a year off and pursue hobbies or creative interests and so share round the community the benefits of both employment and unemployment? If we decide that, we ought not just to see the lack of jobs for everyone as a major problem. If we are creating the prosperity for a smaller workforce to also maintain with social security those for whom there are no jobs, this could be a social opportunity to give a real benefit to many people who could use a free year.*

A young husband whose job demands so much of his time and energy that he has almost none for his wife and children could, under such a system, take a sabbatical year to build a new relationship with his wife and children. Creative energies like writing the book you often say you would if you had the time, or freedom to investigate an idea that has come to you at work but which the normal pressures of life prevent you from going into—these can flower on sabbatical leave. If the system can work well for some university teachers, doctors and clergymen there is no reason why it could not and should not be more widely adopted as a fruitful way of dealing with the problem of too many people chasing too few jobs.

LOW PAY

The second point is that we ought to admire enormously those lower paid workers who conscientiously work even though they know they could be better off unemployed. There must surely be a crisis of conscience for any man who sees his wife and children going without adequate food, clothing or warmth because his pay packet does not provide enough for the family to live comfortably. It is bearable to your self-respect to do your best and yet not provide a sufficient wage to meet the real needs of your family, but hardly bearable at all if you know you could make them all more comfortable by being unemployed. This is an anomaly by which firms who pay low wages to their workers sour a man's motivation and self-discipline.

The issues in this chapter, and many other areas of concern at work, are matters which must lay a responsibility on every Christian worker to take up and try to take action upon. The whole area of work is not some ghetto to be regarded as shut off from the love of God and the insights of Christianity. Through the narrowness of bigoted attitudes, closed minds and entrenched positions there needs to blow the wind of the Spirit. We can open doors and windows in people's minds (and in our own) for that Spirit to blow through. We can bring healing to the scores of damaged relationships, misunderstandings, conflict and opposition. We can prod the settled comfort of those who would rather not notice awkward questions of injustice nor have challenged a philosophy of life that treats only certain people as truly human.

For this task we draw our inspiration and strength from God, our Christian faith and worship, the support, prayers and encouragement of our fellow Christians. In the encounters we seek to relate our theology to the matters of the moment, and to do this we shall need constant help in understanding more thoroughly the Biblical insights of our faith. Clearly this calls the Church to re-examine its purpose and priorities in order to help us its members to fulfil ours at work.

5

HEALTH AND WHOLENESS

HEALTH is a matter of crucial and personal importance to every one of us. It makes many of us uneasy that our local General Practitioners and our hospitals are severely overworked in these days of warmer and more comfortable homes, less physically dangerous work and richer diet. The problem of illness seems to have increased rather than decreased. We have become conditioned to think of immediate treatment and cure for any ailment. We think more about curing ailments and diseases rather than promoting the health of the whole person.

Michael Wilson in his book *Health is for People* (Darton, Longman & Todd £1.95) calls upon us to question the assumptions we make about illness and wholeness in society today. Our preoccupation with chemical and surgical treatment, and the fact that the Ministry of 'Health' is concerned not with promoting health but reacting to 'disease, handicap, death and ugliness' (p. 6) rests upon what we believe about human life. We are now getting many problems because we are over-treating our bodies with so many chemicals. Far too often the treatment is not a real search for the social, physical, emotional and spiritual health of a person in the way they live, their personal discipline, their personal relationships and beliefs, but in simply prescribing a chemical substance to alleviate or cure a symptom.

My own local doctor reckons that more than half the people who come to see him in his surgery come with a problem that is spiritual in origin—it stems from things they believe, how they react to other people, or their lack of morale. We are losing our way in our search for health, and true humanness if we accept that a human being is no more than the sum of his physical and chemical properties, so that any ailment must be given a pill to put it right.

In my own pastoral work as a parish priest I find many people who live under stress. They cannot really relax. Many cannot sleep well; they get depressed. An astonishing number are regularly taking tranquillisers. Their illness stems from things like guilt feelings, bad relationships with people at work or at home, a row with their neighbours, disappointment at the way a friend has treated them. Perhaps they feel inadequate, insecure, angry, jealous, envious, afraid, lonely or just generally dissatisfied with life. The body's reaction to this spiritual malaise can produce reactions like asthma, skin diseases, insomnia, ulcers, angina, constipation, headaches, and may affect the normal workings of eyes, ears, kidneys, digestion and other organs, and may produce pains anywhere that come and go and cannot be easily identified. Such spiritual disorders can also contribute to lack of effectiveness and concentration at work, or driving, or in dealing with dangerous things like a fire, a boiling kettle, and lead to accidents in the home or at work. The stress, and the physical discomfort may often in their turn badly affect personal relationships and so the vicious spiral goes on.

Almost certainly the major cause of physical and mental illness lies in our life-style, personal habits, relationships and beliefs. A concern for health must surely begin with a concern to develop beliefs that help to build better relationships, healthier habits of diet, enjoyment and personal fulfilment. This brings attention back to Jesus' saying 'I came that they might have life, and have it abundantly' (John 10.10). Who else but the Christian community can begin to create in your local area a fresh understanding of health, and provide some of the practical means whereby people can be helped towards positive health and not just reaction to ailments?

12. *This whole subject needs to be discussed afresh in the community with local doctors, nurses (whether Christians or not) and ourselves and others of the general public. Frontier groups to explore the present situation and the possible steps towards a better situation can be initiated by us Christians. Particular recommendations which flow from such discussions can be sent to your local Community Health Council.*

HEALTH IS FOR PEOPLE
Michael Wilson's book *Health is for People* offers a considerable amount of very readable material which can provide the basis for such a group to explore. He writes:

'We need to reshape our beliefs about health and our understanding about illness. The reformation of beliefs and attitudes is basic to all other practical suggestions.

'In particular the clinical model of health, based upon a search for health by the eradication of disease, is leading to greater knowledge of disease and more and more costly ventures to prevent or treat it. We as people need once again to be able to choose a style of health which can enhance our humanness both individual and social' (p. 102).

It is also well worth considering most carefully these quotations from his book:

'Health is a positive quality of well-being' (p. 2).

'Health is closely linked to political decisions about priorities—the things in life such as education, transport, food, farming, opportunities for celebration—to which resources of money and manpower will be given' (p. 38).

'Psychiatrists have introduced a new cluster of criteria for the evaluation of individual and social well-being with profound effects on our ideas of health. We must now include interpersonal factors such as

68

acceptance or prejudice, ability to adapt to social change, attitudes to old age and death, and the stability of marriage and family life in our evaluation of the health of a society. These criteria can be seen to contain ethical assumptions' (p. 45).

'It could be that the search for a friend ... is not simply a search for care and relief from anxiety, depression and the symptoms of alienation and loss of identity so rife in Britain, but a search for meaning, for quality of life, for values other than materialist, and for a chance to develop our humanity together, in fact a search for health' (pp. 50–1).

'The language of science alone is insufficient to describe health: the languages of story, myth and poetry also disclose its truth. Any conference on health must be as widely representative of human genius as possible' (p. 60).

'Doctors are authoritative on the subject of illness, but in matters of health carry the same authority as, for example, teachers, mothers and environmentalists' (p. 90).

HEALTH AND BELIEF

'In Europe widespread loss of Christian belief has resulted in a fear of death which has drained the word "health" of its truly human dimension. Because our model of health is shaped by fear of biological death, cure of disease naturally becomes a supreme value: resources for the support and prolongation of life the supreme concern.'

'To become a Christian is not to be separated from other men, but to become aware of our unity with all creation and the family of MAN in a new way. It is to become willing to affirm as my brother and to give my life daily—even unto death—for any man be he/she young or old, healthy or sick, Christian or not, good, bad, white, mad, black, stranger or trusted friend. This is life and health, its denial is death' (p. 72).

'A healthy group of people can tolerate stress: that

is, they are prepared to suffer. Health does not exclude suffering' (p. 74).

'The health of a family, a group, or a people depends upon the sharing of feelings of anxiety and guilt as well as joy and acceptance' (p. 76).

'Health positively includes suffering as a creative way of dealing with hostile and destructive feelings' (p. 77).

'I have simply pointed to the decisive influence of a people's beliefs about good and evil, in the formation of their concept of health and of the way they set out to achieve it. Such beliefs, often unexamined but tenaciously held, have far-reaching consequences in terms of health care and social services, professional training and design of buildings' (p. 84).

'Beliefs have expensive consequences' (p. 85).

'The modern Health Centres are polyclinics shaped by the belief that we achieve health by the prevention, diagnosis and treatment of disease. The buildings shape the beliefs of those who grow up with them and the language of illness becomes their language, until it can actually be difficult, as in Britain today, to speak of health in any other way' (p. 93).

'Healthy people are not primarily concerned with doctors and nurses, but with family relations ...' (p. 93).

'Health may appear in or through illness and suffering. Illness may be a learning experience. A leper settlement may be a healthy community. A hospital ward may likewise be healthy or sick. The possibility of health in these situations depends upon people, professional or lay, who promote the further possibility of health. Nurses, doctors or patients may be creators or destroyers of health among themselves or others. The health of a ward may stem from the influence of a patient, a nurse or a domestic cleaner.'

KEY PEOPLE

'Every community has its key people who listen to, advise and help their neighbours, colleagues or chance acquaintances. They are the kind of people to whom others turn in a crisis. They are the carriers of a society's culture and therefore the actual builders or destroyers of health. They are key people in any attempt to change a society's attitudes or values in relation to health, illness, life and death. They can be the salt that brings out the flavour of a people's life together, if the salt has not lost its savour' (p. 101).

These key people are not top medics or politicians that he is talking about, but ordinary folk like you and me; teachers, neighbours, barmen, bus conductors, the corner shopkeeper, housewives, mothers and grand-mothers, police, parsons, milkmen, anyone who is listened to for advice and help in the minor and major incidents of life.

It is of first importance that we are prepared to challenge, in our own neighbourhood, so many of the unexamined assumptions on which the daily life of ourselves and our neighbours is lived. We cannot challenge them simply on grounds of expediency, for we come back then to short-term pragmatic answers that we can see more and more are leading us no-where fast. The problems we face at the moment have been created simply by doing just this. You and I, in our own neighbourhood can and should challenge the assumptions of life today from our Christian convic-tions about humanness, God and the purpose and meaning of life.

The Duke of Edinburgh has said:

'Until it can be demonstrated that science, tech-nology and economic growth can take the place of religion and provide that essential inspiration and motive which has created all great civilisations in the past, it would appear that our culture is simply free-wheeling on our Christian inheritance.... The very essence of most religions ... is that they provide the only satisfactory alternative to expediency in making judgements and decisions on the important issues which each generation has to face'. (Quoted on p. 107 of *Health is for People*.)

71

Only when a few people begin to want to explore the full implications of our Christian faith applied to our everyday life in our home, neighbourhood, church and place of work can we really begin to create the sort of society we really want. A different understanding of health is of the very greatest importance to us all, and that different understanding can begin to grow in a family, a neighbourhood group, a church, a community. If it does, it will inevitably have long-term effects upon us all—for good.

This to some people will sound like a parson's pipe-dream. How can we change people's basic assumptions, beliefs and life-style? If Weight-Watchers can do it for people who eat too much, and Alcoholics Anonymous can help those who alone cannot help themselves, then we can do something. I believe that the Christians have a crucial role to play here in every neighbourhood in helping people to come to a fresh understanding and experience of health. I offer one or two examples.

RELAX AND FEEL BETTER

13. *In my own neighbourhood, a fellow church member and I offer to the community at large classes in relaxation. This is something any Christian group can consider doing. We advertised on small posters put up in shops and the entrance-halls of high-rise flats, the local library and doctors' surgeries in this way: 'Relax and feel better. If you find life at work or at home has too many strains and stresses, or if you get worked up and tense dealing with people, learn to relax properly and feel better. This improves most people's temper, concentration, general health and ability to cope.'*

The response to these was considerable, and certainly more than we expected. We now realise that we have to rearrange some of our priorities in church life, to provide in our community a service which people are looking for, for which they are willing to pay, and from which they find real benefit. It is a step towards helping people to experience health, and to find a philosophy and style of life which helps us all to enjoy life fully.

At the time of writing we have organised these sessions of relaxation and meditation in groups of four. They last an hour and a quarter each, and start at 8.15 p.m. which gives mothers for example the freedom to feed their family and see the youngest children to bed, and they can come out without getting into an anxious rush. It is also easier for day workers, but it unfortunately does provide problems for some shift workers who start at 10 p.m. and have a journey of longer than twenty minutes.

FIRST SESSION

At the first session everyone sits on an ordinary hard chair. These are well spaced out in the hall so that everyone sitting can stretch their arms and legs out, without touching anyone else doing the same. We begin with a friendly welcome, and talk about stress and its effect on people's bodies and minds. Then briefly we give examples of tenseness—tightly gripping the steering wheel of the car in a traffic jam, or tossing and turning unable to sleep because your mind is a whirl of activity. Many times in the day you can realise just how tense you are (without being normally aware of it) by deliberately checking how relaxed your shoulders or face muscles are.

We then relate the problems of the character, soul, personality—call it what you will—to the body, and explain that simply relaxing the muscles will not get to the root of tension. The root is spiritual. The point is made but we do not labour it. The meditation sessions touch spiritual nerve ends, and most people then come to see the point for themselves.

The first exercise is deep breathing, to fill the lungs as much as possible, hold it, then gently breathe out to thoroughly empty the lungs. We normally only use a small part of our lung capacity in day to day activity.

Deep breathing feeds the blood stream with more oxygen, which is good for our whole system, particularly the brain. Deep breathing is practised either sitting or standing. Then everyone has the chance to relax again, and chat easily with his neighbours between the two or three short sessions of deep breathing exercises.

The hall is warm, and people are dressed comfortably without heavy coats. They are invited to take their shoes off—it is up to the individual. Then sitting erect in the chair, with back straight, head erect, both feet on the ground, hands resting in the lap or hanging limp at the side, we all go through gently and slowly the process of tightening pairs of muscles starting with the toes, and working up systematically to all the muscles of the face and head. Then they are invited to concentrate on the quiet rhythm of their breathing for a few minutes, before gently coming back to an unrelaxed state!

There is time for a little general chat, and we invite relaxers to say what they think about the exercises. Then we begin again, deep breathing, all-muscles tightening and relaxing, leading into meditation—eyes closed, complete stillness, and the first task is to try and think of nothing, to make the mind a complete blank, during the silence which lasts about two minutes or so. Then we move on to think of one word—God—not to try and make a mental picture of God, just to concentrate on the name. Silence. Then move to a shape, the individuals each choose their own. Silence. Then the teacher gives phrases like 'Peace, be still', or 'My peace I give to you', and there is a silence after each one. Finally, everyone is invited gently in their own time, taking as much time as they like, to come out of the relaxed state.

They then have a short time to comment on their experiences during the session, and we emphasise the importance of stilling the mind in order to be in touch with the spiritual power of God which we normally block out because of the busyness of all our thoughts and activities. Everyone is asked to bring a rug, blanket or something similar next week to lie on.

LATER SESSIONS

The second, third and fourth sessions always include deep breathing exercises (either while standing, sitting or lying) and the relaxation exercises are done on the floor. Different positions for being in a relaxed state are explained and demonstrated. These include lying flat on your back, or on your side in a position often recommended to pregnant mothers at ante-natal classes, or the folded position (like a baby in the womb), knees and face on the floor, or the yoga lotus position. Most people prefer lying flat on their back, but always the choice is their own, and a few people choose to sit on the hard chair.

In teaching these exercises we gradually shift the emphasis from everyone doing every exercise following our instructions and timing, to explaining the exercise and then all of them do it in their own time and their own preferred position. We leave longer and longer times for relaxation and for silence. In the meditations too the periods of silence lengthen. Many people are astonished to realise how long they have been quiet and relaxed on a hard wooden floor, yet perfectly comfortable and thoroughly refreshed by the process.

The second session takes the meditation a stage further than the first. With everyone lying down, completely relaxed, and the lights in the hall out, just one candle flickering as a focus for those who choose to keep their eyes open, people are asked to picture in their mind one person whom they find it hard to forgive. Alternatively, if they cannot think of one, to think of someone they think finds it hard to forgive them. They are urged to think of this person in very black terms, even if need be with hatred. Step by step through the meditation, with pauses for the quiet reflection, we try to understand why they hurt us so deeply, and

75

we walk (in our mind's eye) with them to the Cross of Christ. At the Cross we see the blackness of that person being shed like Pilgrim's Burden of sin in Pilgrim's Progress at that Cross, and we hold hands with the other person and walk with them into Resurrection light and a new relationship. They still bear the scars of the old bitter relationship and so do we (as Christ's scars were visible after his resurrection) but now there is new life in Christ.

The third week the meditation explores the theme of Acceptance. God accepts us just as we are, warts and all. We want other people to accept us, with our weaknesses and our strengths, but we cannot always accept our own, and we certainly find it very difficult accepting other people's weaknesses and strengths. In the meditation we are helped to accept ourselves as we are, other people as they are, God as he is. We look at the new relationship that is possible in Christ between God and us, and between ourselves and other people.

The fourth meditation concentrates on Communion, the one-ness possible with God and with other people. Many other themes we can and do use. They are all means of helping us move towards deeper and more loving relationships, a more relaxed yet disciplined life-style, and discovering something of the spiritual life. For so many people these exercises bring a completely fresh understanding of Christian life, spirituality and relationships.

COUNSELLING AND CARE
They lead too into requests for counselling and help in coping with many personal problems like bereavement and chronic anxiety. The meditation does not necessarily in one evening set an individual off in a completely new life-style and set of relationships, but it has clearly helped many to see that there is another way of living, that it is possible to begin to explore the spiritual life, and that faith in God is for living not for locking up in an ecclesiastical building.

We do not only use formal relaxation exercises, and meditations in the mind based on words. A way for example that we have used to introduce the theme of acceptance is to ask everyone in the room to find a partner they do not know. Then one partner with eyes closed is led by the other round the room avoiding obstacles and other couples. The experience of acceptance and trust from this simple game helps many people to fresh insights into the meaning of these two words through the physical experience of being led—and leading—by the hand, and trusting the other person with your safety. It is a simple exercise, but this, and others like it, opens doors for some people which were closed for them before.

I have introduced the silence and briefly conducted meditation into the Parish Communion service during Lent, and found that within a very short time, the change of physical posture—alert, erect in the pew, yet relaxed and concentrating—and the atmosphere of peace and stillness that soon prevailed, permeated the whole of the service and many people were deeply thankful for this experience. It meant having a much shorter sermon, no creed or gloria, very simple intercessions, one less hymn (and some others shortened if they were too long), but that fitted the mood of simplicity for Lent.

FESTIVALS AND LIFE

14. *Similarly we can use simple physical things to touch off new ways of thinking, new relationships, and a stimulating way of relating the festivals we celebrate in church with the business of living day by day. On Passion Sunday for example (two Sundays before Easter) everyone who comes to church can be given a nail. Yes, an ordinary three-inch nail from the iron-mongers! They are asked to carry it round in their pocket until Good Friday, and every time they feel it there to remember it was human sin (which we all have) which crucified the Son of God who came to be our Saviour. He has taught us to pray 'Forgive us our*

77

trespasses as we forgive those who trespass against us.'
Use the time between Passion Sunday and Good Friday
to heal every quarrel you can, and to make a particular
point of apologising to anyone with whom you are on
bad terms.

We may get such overtures thrown back at us, if so we know that this too is part of our Christian calling, but we must forgive. To emphasise this ourselves we can write on a piece of paper the names of any people we have fully forgiven during these twelve days, and placing them in an unmarked sealed envelope on the bare altar in church on Good Friday we lay them at the cross of Christ. On Holy Saturday the envelopes can all be publicly burnt, so that on Easter Day we rejoice fully and gladly from our own experience of new life, resurrection life, through the ordeal of Christ in which we have tried to share in order that we too may bring abundant life to ourselves and others.

There are so many ways in which we Christians can further a search for wholeness and health in our local community. The Church has a long experience and ministry through confession and forgiveness, the celebration of festivals, the sacraments of Holy Unction (anointing with oil, prayer, and the laying on of hands for the healing of body, mind and spirit), the Holy Communion, the fellowship of love, the care and social life it has created, and the principles of love, compassion, generosity, forgiveness, service and so on which it has taught. Now is not the time to apologise for them because few people seem to want these things. Now is the time to exercise flexibility and imagination in the way we offer them.

CREATIVE THINKING AND EVANGELISM

One of the things modern commercial and industrial managers are taught is Brainstorming and Creative Thinking. You define the problem or the thing you want to do, then everyone in the group is asked to suggest as many ways as possible of solving the problem. These are both sensible and ridiculous, as practical or apparently impracticable as possible; the leader writes every one down. He may prod the group when they have got thirty-five different suggestions, by asking for fifty suggestions so they push their imaginations to the limit to reach this target. Then he may choose two or three including one of the most outrageous ideas, and invite the group to suggest ways of implementing them. Through the whole process there so often emerges, especially with an able group leader, original thinking that has been prodded into action. So many new products, methods and disciplines of work that we regard nowadays as simply applied common sense have cropped up through brainstorming sessions. There is no reason why the Devil should have all the best tunes (as General Booth said) nor all the best ideas.

15. *If we are willing to be imaginative and flexible, we too can—perhaps with the help of a local manager who has some experience of running brainstorming sessions (whether he is a Christian or not)—surprise ourselves by coming up with ideas of using new ways to convey old truths through creative thinking sessions about local community and church life.*

This I think is important to grasp, for when Christians in Britain seek to share the Good News of Jesus Christ with other people, we normally expect folk to respond in a recognisable and traditional way. We may invite them to 'commit their lives to Christ', or join the worshipping community in their local church. For some people, perhaps those coping with heavy burdens of stress at work or at home, inner tensions and anxieties, seriously damaged personal relationships with someone dear to them, they may find as many have that a service like the Eucharist or Evensong does not touch them, ease them, lift them, or comfort them in the way they had expected. It may well be a long time before they are ready to make their own commitment to Christ. Like many of those mentioned in the Gospels who turned to Christ, they have turned to him to find

79

healing, rest, forgiveness, release, acceptance but are not yet prepared to walk with him the Way of the Cross.

They may want to respond to his invitation, 'Come to me, all who labour and are heavy laden and I will give you rest. Take my yoke upon you, and learn from me; for I am gentle and lowly in heart, and you will find rest for your souls. For my yoke is easy, and my burden is light' (Matthew 11.28–30 Common Bible). But we must not too readily equate responding to Christ with participating in only one form of Christian worship and fellowship. It may be that they will come to value deeply the language, the meaning, the experience of liturgical worship, and find it cleansing, renewing, invigorating, true soul-food and true communion with God and their fellow Christians. Equally many may not find themselves on this sort of wavelength for a long time, or ever.

Our forms of worship have been fashioned by the needs and ideals of the monastic orders over fifteen or more centuries (or in the case of the Free Churches by the demands and ideals of the Reformation 400 years ago). I do not want to ignore them, or sweep them aside, for I value them deeply in the form they have come to us and been re-formed in our own generation, but I recognise that they do not seem to meet the needs of many people who have deep inner spiritual longings, conflicts of soul, who are searching for peace, health, mystery, harmony with the Divine. These people seek Salvation, but they may never put it in those words. They seek Christ, but they may not see in the life and worship of the church a way to salvation.

Perhaps they see a building encumbered with childhood experiences of boredom, or harsh treatment received from a former parson or Sunday School teacher or ordinary church member. They hear traditional words which register no relevance or real meaning in their minds. Perhaps because they cannot share belief in the whole faith they feel unworthy or unable to share worship, membership and commitment with those who they believe have a serene faith unclouded by doubt, despair or mistrust. Some simply do not see how liturgy helps anyone to a deeper experience of God; others are content with the pattern of life as they have it now, and only a major disturbance in their life which they do not seek can get them out of a rut and look afresh at the wonder of life as it could be.

EAGLES NOT CHICKENS

Michael Wilson quotes on page 57 *Health is for People* the African fable of the farmer who brought home a chick from an eagle's eyrie and put it with his chickens. It grew up well content with its lot, and when a traveller later took it from the chicken run and said, 'You're an eagle, fly!' it hopped back into the chicken run to peck with them. For more than a week the traveller fed the bird with eagle food to give it the strength to fly, but still it preferred to stay and scratch with the chickens. Not until the traveller took the bird right away from its chicken run to where it had a vision of the glory of the world of an eagle did it stretch out its wings and fly in the fullness of its life and powers.

Many of us who long to share with others the vision of life as it could be in Christ know the frustrations of trying to persuade eagles they are truly eagles with infinite possibilities, rather than chickens who can only scratch about in their narrow contentedness, grumbling about their condition but not wanting to do much to change it. Many church members feel anxious, indeed depressed, because the things we value, and offer to the community at large are widely rejected. We feel hurt, disappointed and uneasy for the future, while we work so hard to maintain the life and traditions we value so deeply. Some of us seem to value the traditions more than the essence of what they seek to express.

Here we must come to terms with our faith, for we see in the Bible time and again that people have chosen almost anything else—Baal worship, the Golden Calf, fertility rites, sheer hedonism, narrow bigotry, slavery in Egypt to freedom in the Promised Land—anything but what God was calling them to. We who are now worried about the financial pressures on the churches, and the shortage of manpower among the clergy, need to realise afresh that in every major change that was for the good of his people, God had to carry them forward kicking and screaming their opposition.

Look at the problems Moses had getting the Children of Israel to follow him to freedom, they moaned about change, about him 'rocking the boat' and up-setting everyone, they were afraid of the Egyptian army, crossing the sea, marching through the desert. They complained about the food, the water and most of the decisions Moses made. Whenever I get fed up because people have criticised me even when I have done my best, I always think of poor Moses and thank God my lot is not as bad as his was.

At the Exile too, no one wanted to believe Jeremiah's words that God was chastening his people by allowing the Babylonians to conquer and destroy their city, and take them captive into Exile for seventy years. These two experiences of Exodus and Exile were deeply formative ones for the Jews. I have no doubt the present experiences will be deeply formative ones for us. Christian maturity comes through suffering. It could well be that being forced to shed some of the load we as an institutional church carry on our backs, we shall be forced to see new ways of expressing Christian faith and life, which will help us to relate the living essence of Christianity to day-to-day living in this new age. I believe that there are signs of this in looking at this whole question of health, spirituality and the meaning of humanness.

16. *To explore this we need to develop what I call 'ecclesiastical schizophrenia'. That is to maintain as basic the traditional elements of worship, spirituality, fellowship and care, but we deliberately create areas*

of time and work in the life of the Church in each area by which we reach out in new ways to help create the sort of society and people we want. This for me is not a dispiriting task, not a defeat, but perhaps a tactical withdrawal before a fresh advance. In the end, we may still use traditional methods but according to a revised plan and a new strategy.

MORALE IN THE LOCAL CHURCH

This of course is a painful process. Already many clergy suffer much from over-work, and are highly sensitive to criticism that they are not doing their job properly. In an article I wrote in 1976 in *ACE*, the quarterly bulletin of the Archbishops' Council on Evangelism I dealt with the problem of lack of morale among many clergymen featuring especially one man who wrote at length his anonymous cry from the heart. One of the many people who wrote to me after that wrote this: 'It was a weird experience for as I read it I kept saying to myself "when did I write this?" So much of it fitted.

'I would like to encourage you to explore this theme more, and maybe bring it to a level of national discussion in the Church. Clergy vary so much as they face this situation—some just get depressed—others say "hold on, all will be set right in time"—others thrash about seeking radical solutions that have a tendency to make people fall off.

'I think one of the problems for clergy is that their role has changed but there are so many pressures to keep it as it was. My parish not long ago had a staff of three, now there is just me. Should I do just a third of the pastoral work or seek to allow my role to change to the bewilderment of the faithful. The parish as such has not learned to receive less, and a month or so ago I was taking seven and eight funerals a week.'

If the Church is to break new ground to focus what it has to offer to society today then many of the traditional structures and patterns of work will have to be broken. If they are not, the Church will less and less meet the needs of people today. If we are to offer creative help to people to find health, and humanness and explore the meaning of life, then time will have to be taken from some of our current preoccupations and given to new ones. This must be a decision shared, agonised over, thrashed out in the local church, for even if we start something in a tentative way on free evenings, we have found at Ormesby that these in themselves build up a demand for more and more time to be given in these ways, which means less and less time for some of the other things.

Members of every local church need to be encouraged to see that nowadays the Church needs to maintain a slimmed-down version of traditional church activities, in order to leave time to explore new ways for Christ. Offering the fruits of Christian spirituality to the public at large (without strings or appeals for commitment), and exploring the role of Christian cells —small groups of fellow Christians who meet in homes or at work—should be recognised as part of the mission of the Church, and possible ways through which God is speaking to us nowadays. Our basic commitment is to Christ, to prayer, to our faith and our fellowship, not to organisational forms we inherited from earlier generations and different circumstances, nor to all our ancient buildings. On the other hand of course, to try and pull up all our roots and create revolution and confusion as a 'necessary therapy for dynamic action' is normally destructive, hurtful and damaging to everyone. The traditional can be slimmed down, as more and more time and effort will be required building up the life and work of the Christian community related to the needs and demands of the present age.

6

COMMUNITY AND FAITH

I AM sure that it is through the local church that significant steps forward can be made to influence individual people, and the community as a whole to a fresh vision of what life is for, and establish communion with Divine Power, and so change the climate of public opinion. The reason why I think the local church (and better still where there are good ecumenical relationships the local churches) can play such a significant part is because the church community is the widest cross-section of age groups, interests and social classes in any community. Young and old, rich and poor, men and women, belong, and the range of their concerns which stem from the teachings of Jesus Christ is as wide as life itself. Every human concern is focused in the liturgy. Folk may sneer at Christian congregations for being middle-class, but in every congregation I have served there have been both wealthy and poor people, working men and women and professional people, and an age range from nine months to ninety years. Many congregations are predominantly middle-class, but any social organisation tends to group itself into those who have a common cultural interest.

On the other hand, the possible range of concerns of the church congregation are wider than any other organisation, for they can include mental health, unmarried mothers, poverty, abortion, battered wives, justice for blacks in South Africa, community relations between different racial groups in our own neighbourhood, community social activities, spirituality, celebration, litter in the neighbourhood, local history, local social work and education, missions, orphans, youth work, care of widowed people, visiting lonely people and so the list could go on. Time and time again when I have asked for support from other organisations in a community for community projects the replies have been evasive because one voluntary organisation will not be associated with a church (its rules say 'no sectarian religion') or a statutory body is bound by the restrictions of the law and cannot go outside the limits of its statutes, or sports clubs say social concern is not their concern, and other organisations decline to operate outside their own speciality. The churches' concerns embrace the whole of life, and they can provide the stimulus in any local community for concerns that are wide and far reaching, and they can be flexible enough in tackling local problems to see life as a whole.

Many of the problems in life today stem from the breakdown of the close-knit community in which joys and sorrows are shared, help is given, compassion is shown, beliefs are shared and reinforced, friendship and laughter are enjoyed. You do not solve the problem of a lonely old person by arranging a visit from a social worker once a week, or simply organising an old people's club every Monday afternoon. The specialist groups and the paid social workers are a very great help, but the real need is to create a richer community life in the local street and neighbourhood. When people live close to friends or family with whom they can share their troubles and talk over their problems, rejoice together over their good news, and help each other bear the burdens of pain and disappointment they do not need so much specialist help. All our excellent helping agencies like Samaritans, Marriage Guidance Councils, Cyrenians (who help feed single homeless people) Gingerbread groups for one-parent families, and so on have arisen to meet the needs people have when local neighbourhood community life has largely stopped, or is very selective.

Christians should certainly give these groups strong support, and much Christian caring work ought to be channelled not through separate church organisations but through them. However, in the long run, we can all add more to the whole quality of life and happiness by trying to develop a real sense of community life in streets and neighbourhoods. There is one street of private houses in my parish where the householders banded together to prevent a block of flats being built at the closed end of the cul-de-sac. Having a common cause to fight for drew them together in a strong bond of friendship, and the strength of friendship once forged has continued in an annual wine and cheese party for everyone in the Close, an annual bonfire party on 5 November and a charity fund-raising carol singing group at Christmas, among other things. There is a willingness to help each other there, just as strong, supportive and enjoyable in a different way as the community feeling in the back-to-back terrace house streets in the centre of Middlesbrough in the past.

However, in the new council estates in my parish there is not the same bond of community life. There are many reasons for this. Television provides company in your own sitting room without needing to sit at your front door to chat with the neighbours for company. As more women go out to work, and many people feel a stronger link with friends in other parts of the area and go to visit them, the same bond of community spirit does not grow up so quickly in new housing estates. Perhaps it will in time, but in the meantime there are many growing problems of loneliness, unhappiness, anger and frustration. A daughter nursing her elderly parent, a family coping with their mentally or physically handicapped child, the deserted wife, the lonely and shy person who lives alone may find the burden they carry too much to bear. Someone else with a similar problem living in a different area with several friendly and helpful neighbours who talk, and listen, and who give the occasional much-needed break from routine, can cope much better.

Often the reason why little community life develops is because there is no given focus, like a common cause to fight for, or a common project to work on. Perhaps the Christian cause thrives in persecution because the Christians draw so much closer together in caring for each other in opposition to the persecutors.

17. *One particular contribution the church can make in any neighbourhood where there is very little community life is to have coffee parties to which a church member, or a more occasional contact like a person who requests baptism for a child or someone who wants to get married, invites friends and neighbours including some people they do not know very well, to a coffee party in their home.*

It can either be a money raising coffee party for church or other charity funds, or simply as a social event to meet one of the clergy. The clergy then meet many people they would not otherwise meet, but the great thing is the neighbours meet and chat between themselves and from this can grow further contacts and invitations to other houses. The church here is simply providing a reason for meeting, and in doing so often laying the foundation of further long-term community activity especially if these become regular meetings.

From them can sometimes grow concerns about particular local issues, or problems common to most of the people who meet in this way. Sometimes Christian cells can develop from them, but certainly friendships often can, and a real sense of caring between people who hitherto have been complete strangers to each other.

At the time of writing this I am preparing the ground for starting a local pantomime to draw together a wide cross section of the community in a group activity in which friendships will grow and lots of people be drawn into involvement with different aspects of making costumes, props, scenery, programmes as well as acting, singing and dancing. The short-term aim is to enjoy ourselves together, and the long-term aim is to help lay the foundations of community involvement,

88

friendship and participation, mixing people who live in different areas of the parish, and mixing people who share our Christian convictions with those who do not.

I am also planning a carnival for a year hence, with the purpose of providing a means in the community for folk to come together working on a common project, which in itself will break down barriers of suspicion and resentment, and join together in joy and celebration. A key principle is to encourage local street committees so that neighbours are encouraged to come together planning their street entry in the Carnival procession and the competition for the best decorated street. The procession itself is intended as a common focus in which entries from the eight separate geographical areas in the one parish can mingle together and all identify as a common community. I hope the street committees will lay the foundation for long-term street community life, for all sorts of contacts and friendships can grow from them, and the whole parish Carnival procession will bring together folk who would not normally come together in any other way.

18. *Every church has an obvious reason for originating the idea of a Carnival in a community, to celebrate a Christian festival like Whitsun or St George's Day or Ascension Day or whatever. The religious festival provides an obvious focus for celebrating religious ideas, and sharing them in a quite natural way in the community. Badges and stickers with 'Smile, God loves you' printed on can pick up a theme which can be continued in other ways with slogans like 'Love God. Love each other', 'Thank God. Thank each other', 'Speak to God. Speak to each other', and 'God cares for you. Care for each other', 'God forgives you. Forgive each other'.*

Community celebration has always been an important feature of religious life, but one that in recent years in this country we have tended to shut within the walls of our church buildings. The religious ideas expressed in those slogans are important to stress in a happy and relaxed way, for the fact that people come together to work on a community project to create fun and celebration doesn't mean there won't be strained relationships, tensions, misunderstandings, rows and folk falling out. There may well be a touch of this, and this provides the obvious testing ground for Christian conviction, to overcome hurt pride and introduce forgiveness, reconciliation and harmony. It provides us with a chance to show that Christian values can bear suffering yet overcome sin, it is tough, it is demanding, and it is a better way of living than taking umbrage and refusing to speak to the person who offended you.

The community life that can grow through such co-operative work can lay the foundation for a richer and happier life-style for so many people in the community, and that must be our long-term aim.

CHRISTIAN COMMUNITIES

19. *There is too an important place in any neighbourhood, whether city, town, suburb or village for those Christians who feel drawn to live together in a community to do so. Like the yeast in the dough such communities can influence the neighbourhood with a vision of shared life, common concerns, Christian values and a working out in day-to-day living of the principles of Christian conduct St Paul puts before us in Romans 12–15.*

Michael Harper in his book *A New Way of Living* (Hodder 50p), describes the Christian communities in the parish of the Holy Redeemer, Houston, Texas. In Britain now there are many small Christian communities and 'enlarged families' experimenting with a Christian life-style that offers a clear alternative to the life-style and expectations of so many of us today. Some families form a type of enlarged family life in their own neighbourhood without sharing one house, but living close to each other, sharing each others joys and sorrows, bound together by common faith and convictions, prayer and celebration, and providing a means of enriching the quality of life for all of them.

Some individual families witness simply to their neighbours to a different set of values and ideals in family life just by being there in the neighbourhood, reaching out and making welcome in their own home any of the neighbours who respond in friendship, and sharing with them their own faith and convictions in ordinary casual conversations.

Any Christian family who wants to, can witness to different values and life-style from the commonly accepted ones which are doing damage to the emotional and spiritual health (and in turn to the mental and physical health) of so many people. It requires in the first place some real concern and conviction that the values and life-style of today fail to offer to us the fullness of life which Christ offers. It then needs an anchor in a lively Christian congregation, and a basic knowledge of Christian theology and prayer, and a personal commitment to Christ. The local congregation should in any case be nourishing these things in all its members.

20. *Any and every Christian family can and should try to show by the quality of life and love, joy and sharing, celebration and happiness, by how they cope with disappointment and suffering, how they help others, by their convictions and behaviour at work and in the community that in this family there is a strength of Christian love which points to there being more in life than most people find.*

SHARING OUR FAITH

We Christians must be bold enough to share our faith with the community at large on a give-away basis. For many years people have said to me that they are Christians but they see no need to come to church. I have been sold on the need to stress the importance of

Church membership, and I certainly believe that the life of the Church is an essential element of full Christian experience, and the fellowship of other Christians is an enormously valuable support and encouragement in living the Christian life. I have tended to illustrate this with the story I heard long ago of the Vicar visiting a parishioner who had stopped coming to church for some time, and now thought that he didn't need to attend church to be a Christian. They were both sitting beside an open coal fire on this winter afternoon, and the vicar picked up the fire tongs and took a brightly burning piece of coal out of the fire and placed it on its own in the hearth, without saying a word. The two of them sat there in silence and watched as the bright flame on the single piece of coal grew smaller until it disappeared into a wisp of smoke, and the parishioner looked up and said, 'I take your point.'

While I think it is of the very greatest importance for Christians to join together in fellowship and support, and for each of us to regularly join in the sacramental life of the Church, there are many people for whom these things have little or no significance yet who do believe in God, have some belief in Christ and prayer and life after death, and whose faith is a good deal mixed with mere sentiment, and convictions which are the opposite of those Christ taught. I believe we Christians have an important task to share our faith with such people in a popular fashion, for many children are now growing up without a moral, spiritual and religious anchor. We are unlikely to get many of them into active Church membership, but we can still hope to influence their values, convictions and personal practises with Christian teaching.

21. *Phrases like 'God is good', 'He's gone to a better place', 'prayer works', 'God bless you', and Christian songs like 'The Lord's my shepherd', 'Amazing Grace', 'Morning has broken' and 'Day by day' among others*

have sunk into the mental library of many ordinary non-churchgoing people and shape some of their beliefs and actions. Such people may never normally come to church, yet these are some of the religious guideposts of their lives. It is through community celebration, popular music, attractive stickers and posters, the choruses and other songs we get adults and children to sing that folk religion can still be taught in Britain today. They certainly need supplementing, with phrases on forgiveness, sin, God at work in our lives, and seeing Christ in each other, but they are an important means with which we can counter-attack modern secularism.

In the Gospels we see Christ doing just this, offering to the crowds at large his teaching on God and life and behaviour, offering healing, gathering communities, sharing sorrows and joys and bidding people live by his teachings. This is popular teaching, not systematic theology, and it is popular teaching to the community personally not through the radio or the parish magazine. It is the sort of thing that can circulate through the pubs, club, works canteen as well as the 19th hole, the cocktail party and the luncheon club.

We have a public relations job to do for God, to get something of his Word across to the wider community, and to do this we must make it simple and easily digestible. More often than not we shall not see the response in additional church membership, but the hidden response in people's minds and private actions is something we can just hope and pray for even though we shall rarely see the results of it. I have a strong feeling that with a great many people, their doubts about religious teaching stem more from the fear that they are out of step with what most people think, than with honest intellectual doubt.

That is simply a fashion of thinking we have at the moment. As I have said before, fashions change and we can help change them. Through popular and simple religious teaching, and often presented through involvement in secular community life, I believe we can do an important evangelistic job of sowing seed that we may not see growing and we may never harvest.

Just as local shopkeepers dread the visit of the pushing salesman, and many of them deliberately refuse to buy as much as they might otherwise do simply because he pushes them so hard that they see their self-respect at stake in refusing to be pushed, so the Church has an image as a pushing salesman. Folk don't mind us sharing our beliefs, but its being pulled within the web of the ecclesiastical spider that they buck at. Talk about our beliefs by all means, but really people have to want to respond themselves, either because what we do seems to them to have some meaning and importance and enjoyment, or because they see what a difference it makes in our lives.

22. *It is through living our faith in the market place of life, not entirely shut up in the holy shrine—but certainly the faithful draw their strength from the worship, fellowship, teaching and sacramental life focused in the holy shrine—that we can most powerfully and attractively show the relevance and unique power and alternative life-style of Christ to our bewildered, unhappy and materialistic society. In the recent past the church has either tended to get wholly involved in community work and been shy about Christian faith, values and beliefs as anything distinctive, or else it has fostered the 'come ye out' philosophy of having as little as possible to do with secularism. We have got to be the Christian yeast in secular dough, and the Christian salt that adds its particular flavour to whatever it is mixed with.*

But both yeast and salt can only do their most effective job if they are thoroughly—yet distinctively—mixed in with the whole community life and work. Dough that apologises for being dough and tries to pretend it is flour and water would be useless and the mixture would turn out soggy and flat. Salt that pretended not to be savoury would likewise be of no value at all. So too, yeast in its packet is not active in the dough, and salt in the jar achieves nothing at all. If we Christians believe we have something distinctive in belief and life-style to contribute to community life in Britain today then we must see to it that we introduce this distinctiveness in every part of life, and we give to our own local community our active service in trying to create the sort of society we want our children to grow up in, and in suggesting the sort of people we need to be to achieve that sort of society.

FRONTIER GROUPS

23. *This brings us again to the importance of frontier groups. The local church is the ideal community to foster such important meeting points between people across the different frontiers of their own sectional interests. It may be one of the most valuable things a church could do to bring together local doctors, social workers, police, probation officers, schoolteachers, clergy, councillors, play schools and organisers of pensioners' clubs, youth leaders and others in common concern for the well-being of the whole community.*

Often one group does not realise what others are doing, or how the areas of concern overlap. Sometimes a family may be visited by many of these people, yet the people visiting never meet each other. Such a wide cross section of people may make a useful occasional gathering for exchange of opinions, but a smaller selection of about eight people is more likely to provide a really useful working group and exchange of opinions.

24. *Again the churches can foster the drawing to the attention of people in the whole community, not just church members, of the needs of organisations like Samaritans, Marriage Guidance and others for volunteer helpers, and of the need to support caring and support agencies like Alcoholics or Gamblers Anonymous.*

Perhaps only the churches, one local church, or a group, or a Council of Churches can draw together from time to time a Community Conference involving statutory bodies from local councils, with local volunteers, and organisations like the schools, youth clubs, Rotary, Women's Institute, Townswomen's Guild, Round Table, National Housewives Register, Scouts and Guides, councillors, tradesmen and professional people, Community, Tenants and Ratepayers Associations and others to consider deep local problems or needs. So often a big fuss and a public meeting stem from some short-term crisis, whereas it is often the longer deeper lying problems that nobody wants to tackle but from which we all suffer.

In the blessing at the 1928 confirmation service, the Bishop bids us 'Hold fast that which is good, render to no one evil for evil, strengthen the fainthearted, support the weak, help the afflicted, honour all. . . .' Clearly the sort of society we want is one in which we do everything we can to fulfil those injunctions. Yet in every community people, ourselves included, complain again and again about people like councillors, local government officials, deliverymen, shop assistants and almost everyone who comes into contact with us at different times. Time and again anyone in the public eye only knows what folk think about them and their work when they are being criticised. Now this is just not fair, and gives no encouragement to good work. A person who is never praised for good work, but pilloried for a mistake or a piece of bad work, will soon tend not to try too hard about anything feeling there is no incentive to give of their best. This is another current fashion of thought that we have become stuck with, and the local church can do something about it.

25. *We can encourage in our prayers, publicity, and personal encouragement to get folk to give thanks for the service given to us by councillors, milkmen, roadsweepers, nurses, school teachers, policemen, doctors,*

parsons, good neighbours, coalmen, crossing wardens,
shop assistants and others. Publicly encourage people
to give public service by recognising and appreciating
that service and by public esteem. To get the best out of
most people you need both a carrot and a stick, en-
couragement and criticism: feed them on the thistles
of criticism only and you sap enthusiasm and good-
will, and you get a poorer performance than you
otherwise might.

CHURCH AND COMMUNITY

In some communities, some of these activities of
carnival and celebration, community care and discussion of issues, are already flourishing thanks to the
activities of organisations other than the churches.
That's fine, thank God for it. The churches ought not
to stand aloof from such activities, but through individual church members who participate and official
Church Council representatives the local churches
ought to be involved if possible. Through such
activities we can relate the things we believe in to the
joys and cares of our local community and hope to
win acceptance for the fact that the Christian faith
offers particular guidance on the philosophy of life
by which we should seek to frame our decisions. The
community at large may not share our convictions,
but it is important, with goodwill, humour and tact
on our part that they come to accept that we can work
together even if we disagree on a philosophy of life,
and that the Christians hold by a philosophy and faith
which offers an alternative to modern current assumptions.

Perhaps in many places the Church begins something which others take up and develop. We need to
learn the wisdom to know the difference between
holding fast to a principle which is right, and the
obsessive refusal to hand over to someone else simply
because we take a pride in having started something
valuable.

7

CHURCH AND
NEIGHBOURHOOD

THE Archbishops' 'Call to our Nation' must be trans-
lated by the local church to a 'Call to our Neighbourhood'. What sort of neighbourhood do we want? What
sort of people do we need to be to achieve it? The
greatest danger it seems to me that Christian groups
can fall into is to spend hours and hours wisely chew-
ing the cud on national and world problems, only to
come to the conclusion there is nothing that our little
group of dedicated church members at Much-Binding-
in-the-Marsh can do about it. The group discussions
have been very stimulating and interesting, and we all
go home and carry on as before. We see the need for
change, but somebody else must initiate the changes.
Rubbish! If we see the need for change, we can make
a start by changing ourselves—even if we are the only
ones in step—and we can start to talk about the need
for change, with the intention of building up a new
climate of public opinion. For most people, change
on a national or international scale we reckon is beyond our ability. Well we cannot expect overnight to
walk the world's stage, but we already walk on our
own local stage and it is here that we can make a
definite contribution by responding to the Archbishops' 'Call to our Neighbourhood'.

In any local community, whether city, town or
village, it is possible for a group of people with vision
and courage to create a change in public opinion in
their own community, and introduce practical expres-
sions of that changed opinion, and so set patterns
which may have a snowball effect which others take
up. Local issues are what get people going more than

national ones. Anyone who travels round the country will know that the whole feeling of community life can change considerably from one area to another, just as the accents are different. We may live in what Marshall McLuhan has named the 'Global Village' and be aware of what is happening in Johannesburg, New Delhi, Washington, Sydney, Paris, Beirut, Lima and Peking but still the issues that really get us going are next door's kids, the local water rate, the workmate with a chip on his shoulder, the publican who doesn't really make an effort to attract custom, the social worker who is rude and unhelpful, the potholes in our road, the local vandals and the cutback in local council services.

The problem of battered wives, or soldiers killed in Northern Ireland, or the national figures for unemployment, burglary or road accidents do not seem real until the problem comes home to us in our own street and neighbourhood. It comes powerfully when we know well someone who has been battered, or killed, or unemployed or burgled, and most powerfully of all when it happens to us or a member of our family.

So it is important for Christians in a neighbourhood to make a positive response to local issues and problems. If what you do in your neighbourhood is good, you may well find people from other neighbourhoods coming to borrow your ideas and experience, and your actions can have a snowball effect and influence other communities.

People in many walks of life travel these days to the oddest corners of the world, to apparently insignificant neighbourhoods and out-of-the-way villages to look at good ideas which a small group of people have tried and which have offered a pattern for many others to follow. One example, for instance, is the magnificent effort made in a lonely Irish village community at Cape Clear Island off the coast of West Cork in the Irish Republic. There the local Catholic priest has done something constructive to prevent his community from dying. He persuaded the islanders to turn themselves into a company, and persuaded the Government to bring work to Cape Clear. The Co-operative idea for a whole rural community has been taken up elsewhere, for instance at Glencolumbkille in West Donegal, and at Llanaelhaearn, Gwynedd, North Wales under the leadership there of the local doctor, Carl Iwan Clowes. He and a friend visited Cape Clear Island, learnt from them, then in their own village formed the Villagers Association and the village Co-operative, entitled Antur Aelhaearn. (Antur means venture, and Aelhaearn the name of the saint who founded the village in the sixth century.) Its aim is to keep the village community alive (they fought for the retention of the village school) by providing housing, amenities, services and above all work in the area. Over three-quarters of the villagers are now shareholders in the venture, and they have combined together to provide a new centre in the village costing £15,000 which now houses a small knitwear factory, a pottery and an outlet for their produce.

In addition Antur Aelhaearn has improved the social life of the area with Eisteddfodau, dramas, film shows and concerts promoted by the villagers on a scale unknown previously. Antur Aelhaearn has received considerable notice throughout the western world as a mode for rural survival.

The world has beaten its paths to tiny communities for their good ideas, whether to Clun or Swaledale for their breeds of sheep, Wensleydale and Cheddar for their cheese recipies, Aylesbury for their breed of ducks or Kendal for its mint cake. A lively Christian community, with faith and compassion, prayer and service, love and idealism can be a beacon of hope to the community in which it is set, and can truly become the yeast that leavens the dough, and the salt that savours the dish.

We may be hamstrung by the strength and rigidity of conservatism within the congregation, and by the almost overwhelming financial and administrative demands of the institution, the buildings and the diocesan quota, but I still believe it is possible for even a small group of people to come together, think, pray, talk and work together to make even some small progress towards creating the sort of neighbourhood we want our children to grow up in, with the vision of what human life is for, a striving for both community and personal flowering of human potential, for love and justice, for enjoyment and friendship, grounded in the faith, teaching and experience of Jesus Christ. It is possible to create a new climate of opinion, and a new pattern of behaviour, and we can start within the fellowship of our own local church.

THE PURPOSE OF THE CHURCH

It is of crucial importance for each church to be clear what its purpose is. By each church, I mean the local congregation. In some congregations the real purpose is to maintain the building as a focus for Sunday worship, and most of the effort of time and money raising is to this end. We really ought to ask ourselves whether the church was built to serve the needs of the congregation, or the congregation was gathered to serve the needs of the building. In some congregations the church is the natural and joyful focus of a loving and worshipping community life which contributes significantly to the spiritual, moral, social and caring needs of the community. In others a vast building is like an albatross round the neck of the congregation, sapping its energy, and diverting it from joy, celebration, love and care, to fund-raising to maintain the vicar and his ancient monument.

It will require courage to move out of a building that is too big, or too expensive to maintain, or no longer in the right place, and worship in simpler surroundings or join with another congregation. The wisdom to know what is the right thing to do, and the courage to actually do it, can only come from the strength of our convictions about what the local church's purpose is. I have written more fully about this subject, and our own exercise at St Cuthbert's Church, Ormesby in drawing up a statement of our parish purpose and aims, in *New Ways for Christ* (Mowbrays £1.25, published in 1975). The great value of having written an agreed purpose is that then everybody in the church knows what it is we are trying to do in our Christian life, and people who join us know what our goals are. The purpose as we have defined it reads:

We see our purpose at St Cuthbert's to be a family of people committed to Christ and to each other, who together worship God with joy and love, and seek to be guided and empowered by the Holy Spirit.

We hope to know and to care for each other, to support and encourage each other in a Christian life-style.

We see it as our task to apply our Christian faith and moral values to every aspect of our lives as individuals, and in our family, social, working and community life. We want to bring others to share our Christian life, and so help them to come to a personal experience of Christ, and their own commitment to him.

26. *It is important for every congregation to start with a basic task of working out together, in your own words, and through the valuable exercise of discussing and hammering out the pros and cons of various alternatives, exactly what you see to be the basic purpose of your life together as Christians. It is more important for each church to frame its own words than to copy someone else's words. Only when that is clear will you be able to see how the various possible activities you could be doing can fit into your basic purpose. From there you can go on to define particular aims for the next two or three years, and then set objectives towards which you will work over the next three or six months or whatever.*

Aimless energetic activity will use up a lot of time and manpower, but may get you nowhere: purposeful activity will make much better use of time and abilities, and hopefully will prevent you being sidetracked into all sorts of interesting byways that divert you from your main road.

PRAYER

We all clearly need some priorities about prayer. Too many of us Christians have been lacking in confidence about the practise of prayer and commending it to other people, or teaching it to our own church members. While the Maharishi Yogi has been travelling the world recruiting followers of his Transcendental Meditation technique, and Yoga classes have mushroomed in most Evening Class programmes, the Christians have been so wrapped up in liturgical reform that we have neglected to offer with confidence the teaching and practise of Christian prayer to those who do not choose to join our Sunday congregations.

We tend to commend prayer on theoretical grounds, that it is a Christian duty to be in communion with God, but we can also with confidence commend it on pragmatic grounds that prayer benefits the one who prays and other people. Medical tests on people meditating show changes in the Alpha rhythms, lower blood pressure and shallower breathing which in themselves lead to a more relaxed state of mind, a greater peace and contentment, and a heightened appreciation and sensitivity to people, to beauty and to atmosphere, and often an improved creative ability. People who can be still in body, mind and spirit and have a trust in the care and providence of Almighty God are healthier and happier than they otherwise would be.

We can justifiably draw the conclusion from the evidence presented to us (in Alister Hardy's *The Biology of God* for instance) that work done by Russian scientists and others into telepathy, extra sensory perception and the power of mental thought to influence ourselves, other people and objects, that the mental process of prayer, praise and intercession may in fact be using a biological 'radio' communications system, a spiritual wavelength through which we can draw inner strength from the Supreme Creative Mind—or God as we call him—and through which we can channel such strength to others. We are beginning to feel our way towards a scientifically intellectually satisfying rationale of intercession, and divine healing. Put at its lowest, we can all confirm from our own experience, the truth of William Temple saying to those who regard answered prayers as merely coincidences: 'When I pray coincidences happen; when I don't, they don't.'

27. *To pray for the people of our neighbourhood, our family, our fellow church members, our local councillors and officials, community leaders and those people who are sick, bereaved, in distress, or those who seek wisdom, courage, guidance in important decision making is to make an important and very practical contribution to the sum of health and goodness in our own community. Christians have an important role to play here, to pray expecting to see the fruits of that prayer in changes and improvements in the local society.*

Planned, systematic group prayer, regularly and not just a flash in the pan, which grows from a context of praise and awe and wonder of Almighty God, and a faith that through the power of believing prayer and responsive souls God's spiritual strength and creative energy can be more powerfully at work, is surely one of the priorities for any Christian church. Prayer is a force that can help to heal broken relationships, mellow awkward characters at work or at home, develop wisdom and justice, and give comfort and help.

28. *We must with confidence commend to others, whether they choose to worship with us in church or not, the practise of prayer and meditation. Further-*

*more we ought to offer simple basic teaching, to our
own members and to others, in the practise of prayer
supported by practical justifications which make sense
to people.*

SALTY

I use the word SALTY as a handy mnemonic to teach
people the basis of prayer.

> S is for Sorry: penitence and confession of sin.
> A is for Adore: to express and feel our love.
> L is for Listen: the quiet waiting upon God.
> T is for Thanks: the expression of gratitude and
>   appreciation.
> Y is for Yearn: to want the best for others and for
>   ourselves.

I also suggest that busy people can find a great help
in using a rosary, not with the traditional repetition
of the 'Hail Mary' prayer, but using each group of ten
beads to focus our attention on one aspect of either
penitence, love, meditation, thanks or intercession in
the SALTY scheme. It is possible then with a rosary in
your pocket to pray walking down a street, travelling
in bus or train to work, or quietly sitting for some odd
ten minutes we have to ourselves at any time of the
day. The fact of holding the beads in your fingers
helps discipline the mind and prevent it wandering all
over the place. Sitting in a train, with your hand in
your pocket moving your fingers from bead to bead,
you can pray without advertising the fact, but the very
stillness and peacefulness of your body and mind will
add some influence for good to those around you.

29. *Furthermore we can also think of developing
in the life of the church groups of people to prepare
the liturgical worship for the main Sunday service,
bringing to the lessons, hymns and prayers the width
of their own experiences at work, at home, at leisure,
and in community service.*

Such groups have made a very considerable impression in the life of the Roman Catholic parishes in Holland, creating both a deep sense of lay participation in the liturgy, and focusing the concerns of prayer, praise, Bible study, intercession, confession and celebration very much on to the real issues people face day by day.

Such groups prepare the readings, and discuss them, then prepare the intercessions, choose the hymns, and feed in ideas and comments to the person who will preach. The people involved in the groups then bring to the service a degree of commitment to that service, involvement and reflection on its theme, from which they, the clergy, and the congregation at large greatly benefit. It is possible to gather a group to do one such service every two months or so, and from this hope to develop so that with many groups each working towards a given date for the service they are particularly involved in, more and more of the congregation come to think very carefully through the meaning and significance of worship, and become more involved in it.

In this way, the Sunday worship then becomes a community activity, a corporate act of praise, intercession, penitence, submission to God, inspiration and encouragement in the Christian life, and we see the liturgy as the focus of our life as yeast in the community dough. It is the community's concerns, as well as just the church's concerns, which are offered and submitted to God, for him to bless, forgive and enrich.

We need to pray not just for Clifford our Bishop, but also for Jack our Mayor, for Angela, Joe, Pat, and Doug our Councillors, for John our village policeman and so on. The neighbour in need, the workers being made redundant, the old lady who was robbed and the kids (and their families) who robbed her we need to pray for. Our penitence must not be just for our private sins, but a deep sense of penitence too for the attitudes in society that can accept the foul working conditions some people have to endure, the loneliness and heartbreak which grow out of current public opinion.

The heartaches of deserted families, pregnant single girls, robbed old ladies, and lonely folk pining for company grow out of current assumptions and attitudes which we all have a hand in contributing towards or failing to fight against. Corruption, injustice, laziness and lack of conscientiousness may be built into an organisation and system because the assumptions are not being challenged; too many of us prefer to turn a blind eye. This should be part of our corporate penitence, and lead with a knowledge of God's forgiveness, to seeking strength and courage from him to fight against institutionalised sin.

CHURCH MEMBERSHIP

A clear purpose, and a dedication to praying, are fine to have but they need an organisational focus and discipline to keep up the sense of encouragement, and to get things done and stop ourselves slipping back from our determined objectives. Without some clear structure the ideas merely remain laudable aims we never quite get round to achieving. It seems to me that in Britain today, against a secular background which rejects Christian assumptions, the Christian community has to become a much more self-conscious group of people committed to common disciplines as well as a common faith. The reluctance of top church people to accept this is naturally strong, for the Church of England is the established church, and technically anyone who doesn't belong to someone else's church or religion is reckoned to belong to ours, unless they opt, as very few do, for no religious affiliation at all. Very few people indeed do not have a religious service at their funeral.

Personally I am all in favour of welcoming as many people as wish to come to our church and its services on a casual basis, and I acknowledge that I have a responsibility to serve as many people as I can who ask for the services of the Church. I believe the involvement of church members in every aspect of life and work in a community is very important, but I also see the great need for those who are consciously practising Christians and worshippers at church to have a real sense of belonging to one another, and a disciplined commitment to certain basic obligations. I am a former member of Rotary, and now a member of Round Table. In both these secular, non-religious, non-sectarian organisations, there is a strong sense of community, a basic obligation to the aims of the movement, and a responsibility to put in a minimum number of attendances and to pay a subscription annually to meet the costs of the organisation. Backsliders are chivvied along, but genuine cases of illness or pressure of work or family commitments are treated with great interest, concern and help. Service is freely given to the community at large, and professional standards of integrity and responsibility are stressed. Where members no longer feel able to meet their basic obligations to their fellow members, they either resign, or are invited to think again about their obligations and in rare and extreme cases are notified that their membership has now lapsed. Some of the Free Churches do this, and I feel that we in the Church of England need to consider the value of it.

Look at the other side of the coin. I realised to my horror some months ago that a lady whose face seemed familiar was at church again. She had been away to Australia for nine months, and I had not missed her. Weeks can slip by when members of the congregation are away for many reasons, business, holiday, family commitments, an upset between them and another church member, or they take umbrage at something the clergy have said or done, or they may be ill. One regular member of our congregation was away ill some years ago and no one missed her for three months. This year, since we have introduced the exchange of the Peace at the end of the service after the Blessing, and we encourage members of the congregation to greet and talk to each other, no end of people have asked her husband how she was when she was ill. This is not just an isolated incident. In every church I have worked I have come across people who have quietly dropped out of church membership and no one has noticed, or they have been off ill and no one has visited them. You notice the prominent ones, but the quiet and shy ones can too easily be overlooked.

30. *At Ormesby we plan now to draw up a list of active church members, people who worship with us normally at least once a month. We shall draw up the lists under the service to which they normally come, and include their Christian and surnames, address and telephone number, their work and chief interests. We shall group families together, and where some members of the family do not normally worship with us we shall include their names in brackets. We shall also include the list of people who worship only at house churches, or who receive sick communion. We shall also provide a simple list of names and addresses grouped geographically so that people who come to different services and do not realise a near neighbour also worships with us at a different service can be in touch. A copy of this duplicated membership book will be given to every member. A couple of blank pages at the end will allow space for additions. The list can be revised every two years. Members will be asked to pray and care for each other.*

31. *We plan to organise regular group meetings, perhaps once every three months (or more often if desirable) for a group of church members who live near each other. One family or individual acts as co-ordinator, inviting the others to a coffee-party at which with one or more of the clergy we talk over some of the plans and ideas in church life, raise local community issues and social problems, relate aspects of our faith and Bible study to our immediate concerns, and perhaps pray together. We shall encourage fellow church members to be in touch with each other, to*

notice when one is away and see if all is well, and the clergy aim to look at the list weekly to see who is in church week by week and who is away. In this way we hope not to provide a threatening Big-Brother-is Watching-You survey, but a simple caring check on who is away and to see if they are all right.

The value of the Methodist Class Meeting for church members to meet together, keep in touch with each other, pray, study and plan together, and to be conscious of belonging to each other is of great value. It seems a shame that it is losing its significant place in Methodism.

MONEY

The sense of Christian responsibility for paying for the life and work of the church, the salary of the clergy and so on is something too that can perhaps be fostered through a sense of minimum membership payment. This is the system in the Church of South India. The concept of Stewardship is valuable, but we have to remember that the original concept of Stewardship, tithing, giving one-tenth of your income as an offering to God was also related to spending the money given on works of mercy like education, care of the poor and the sick, as well as maintenance of the church and the clergy. Nowadays, with taxation taking from us a much higher proportion of our income than one tenth for the works of mercy like education, medical and social welfare we ought also to revise our concepts of godly giving. Simply raising money to maintain certain buildings or services which really ought not now to be maintained is not a wise use of money. The concept of stewardship—being responsible to God for the responsible and truly compassionate use of all that we have, is the principle we now need to stress. It ought to be linked with our conception of the purpose of the Church, and our wider responsibilities in works of mercy not covered by government services, and with our sense of responsible help to Christians in other lands for whom financial help from us can be of immense benefit.

32. *There is no reason why the concept of minimum membership payment, with different rates for the average wage earner, the average pensioner and so on, should not be worked out within the congregation. Given the number of committed church members, it ought to be possible year by year for a combined meeting to discuss, pray about, and decide with care, tact and sensitivity over the period of a couple of weeks what ought to be the minimum membership payments for the next 12 months.*

In South India the concept is based on the average wage for three days work. That is the membership payment for the year, and the weekly offering is something on top of that which each individual decides according to his means his sense of commitment, and his conscience. This is something which really ought to be freely discussed widely amongst the congregation, and the lay members themselves taking the main part in deciding what is right to do.

DISCIPLINE

33. *If being a church member really means a sense of commitment and involvement in the purpose of the congregation to which the member belongs, there is a great value in setting down, after thorough discussion as widely as possible among the members, what elements of obligation there rests upon each individual to play their part in furthering that purpose. It can be of the greatest benefit to help a congregation really think through what it is about to be involved in working out both the definition of its purpose, and spelling out the implications of that for themselves in a Common Discipline.*

Many years ago the two Archbishops of Canterbury and York at the time were asked to draw up their Guide to the Duties of Church Membership. This has been widely reprinted in lots of ways and is still available. But to me, a list worked out by two Archbishops 20 years ago is not half as valuable as a concept of common discipleship which friends and fellow church members of each local congregation work out together for themselves, related to the demands, hopes, pressures, anxieties and opportunities of their own situation at the present time. I suggest such a Common Discipline should include individual and corporate obligations, and perhaps could be worked out under these headings which follow.

(A) Prayer. A basic common obligation on each member to an agreed minimum prayer discipline, either daily or weekly. The Muslim has his thrice daily prayer times, and knows that every conscientious Muslim is keeping that time with him. The Catholic Angelus bell at 6 a.m., noon, and 6 p.m. offered a similar common discipline. We have lost the value of that common minimum obligation laid on all our members, which gives every individual the sense of support and encouragement to know that even though he or she may be praying alone it is a practise shared regularly with every other member of the congregation.

(B) Family life. There are surely basic obligations which any Christian has to their own family, and the saddest thing to find is the wife and children of a clergyman suffering from neglect because he is so obsessively involved in caring for everyone else at their expense. Simply to define Christian obligations as 'no divorce' is to offer a negative and impoverished concept of the richness which faith, hope and love in Christ ought to bring to family life. If we are to try and create the sort of society we want, we must hold before ourselves the ideal of the truly Christian family life.

(C) Work. What are the basic Christian obligations at work? In drawing up a Common Discipline we may

want to refer to concepts like justice, conscience, conscientiousness, respect for the humanness of other workers, ethics, and trustworthiness.

(D) *Leisure*. Enjoyment and recreation are an important part of wholesome living, though we must always be mindful not to enjoy ourselves at the cost of hurting other people or ignoring their right to recreation. All work and no play does make Jack or Jill dull, and the earnest puritan kill-joy has done the cause of his Lord and his fellows no good at all.

(E) *Church membership*. The sense of commitment to worship, sacramental fellowship, and sharing with fellow church members in the community life and work and witness of the Church need to be expressed in certain minimum obligations which then all church members feel is accepted by them all. Features like shift work, and visiting parents every third weekend or something are clearly ignored in the slightly unreal world of the Guide to the Duties of Church Membership. Now that house churches or Christian cells meet on days other than Sunday and not necessarily weekly, means that such obligations have to be worked out by each congregation for themselves, according to the local circumstances.

(F) *Christian values*. The study and application of theology to life, the discipline of regularly studying some aspect of Christian faith, whether in an Evening Class, a house discussion group, a lay weekend training session, a retreat, or simply reading a book, watching a television series or listening to a radio programme must be an important part of any Christian discipline. We cannot grow in the Christian life if we do not accept a discipline of regular—even if only once a year for a six week Lent course—refresher or training course in some aspect of our faith.

(G) *Money*. The Christian obligation to use all money wisely, and to accept a responsibility for a realistic payment to the work of the church and to charitable work, clearly needs to be set out in a specific way.

(H) Service to others. The obligations of the Christian to listen to the story of the Good Samaritan and then 'go and do likewise' is one of the clearest obligations laid on us by our Lord. That service may be in kind neighbourly care, in voluntary service as a Samaritan, in a pressure group or trade union, service on a Community Health Council, a District Council, or on a church synod or professional management group committee.

(I) Ministry in the church. St Paul taught his church members to think of themselves as the Body of Christ, with Christ as the head, and everyone of us limbs or organs, so that the whole body is only at its most effective when every limb and organ is doing its own task properly. For everyone of us there is a ministry, a service we can give within the life of the church. It ought to be accepted that every church member on the active membership list should have an area of ministry with a time limit so that there can be a regular change of responsibilities every year or two (depending on the tasks). Such an area of ministry might be sidesmen, or pew polisher, magazine distributor or Sunday School teacher, organist or bellringer, lesson reader, server, sick visitor, rota organiser, book-keeper or whatever. Very busy people will have a minimum task, but everyone ought to have some area of ministry for which they are responsible, and these need to change from time to time to give variety, and so develop a wide range of capable people. It is of course more difficult to change jobs round in tiny congregations but the principle is an ideal no congregation ought to lose sight of.

(J) Bible reading. I put this at the end of the list deliberately. I do so not because it is the least important, for I put all ten aspects as equally important. I put Bible reading at the end, because I see it not as a chore to have to do if you are a Christian, but because I believe that as we Christians seek to pray, apply our

faith in every aspect of our lives, and re-evaluate what it means to be a member of a Christian church, we shall feel stronger and stronger the need to feed on the Bible, to draw strength, inspiration, guidance, and a focus for our lives from its pages. The Bible only really comes to life as you try to relate your own life experience to the teachings of Christ, and as you relate your relationships with God and other people to the relationships of joy and suffering, sin and sanctity which we see in the lives of the Biblical characters.

MINISTRY

All through Biblical history God has used the pressures of political and social circumstances to teach, reform and renew his people in their vision of faithful service to him. He used the traumas of the Exodus and the Exile to shake those eagles who thought they were merely chickens out of their rut and through the painful experiences to come to realise their potential as children of God. Through the pressures of inflation and institutional inertia, it seems God is teaching his children today to renew their vision of what it means to be the Church, how ministry should be exercised within the Church, and what role that Church has to play in the wider community in which it exists. All over the world we find a movement towards a greater sharing of the ministry within the Church.

In the Church of England we find a growing interest in non-stipendiary ministry and training men for ordination who continue in their secular employment after ordination and exercise their ministry in the Church in an honorary capacity. In the Episcopal Church in Scotland, where financial pressures have forced them to reduce their full-time clergy staff by one third in five years, measures taken to train men for the non-stipendiary ministry have now been extended to provide a basic training for ministry for men and women in the Church to equip them to exercise various forms of leadership and ministry in the Church without necessarily being ordained. The former Bishop of Alaska recently resigned to begin a new ministry in the American Episcopal Church fostering the project called TEAM, which stands for Teach Each A Ministry. He visited England in the summer of 1976 pressing the idea here.

34. *A shared teaching and pastoral ministry, a shared ministry of administration, counselling, preaching and liturgical leadership is all possible nowadays with the greatly improved standard of education, the shorter working week for many people, the earlier retirement and redundancy or unemployment. Many people who have been compulsorily retired are very ready to do a useful and interesting job for two or three days a week for two years. Every congregation needs to review carefully every three years or so its ministry and leadership, and decide who should do what, and what changes are desirable.*

Where it is difficult to get responsible and mature people to take Sunday School classes, there is no reason why, if some are willing to give time during the week after school finishes, children should not receive their basic catechism training and Biblical knowledge in a small group of eight to ten children meeting in a home near their own (or their own home) to be taught by one of the mothers for 40 minutes once a week. The programme of work can be linked to the themes of a weekly Family Service at church in which all the families are involved.

A ministry of preparation for marriage or baptism, confirmation preparation, sick visiting, pastoral counselling and so on are all possible. I hope that where a communicant Christian is ill at home, another member of the congregation can in some circumstances take to the sick person the sacrament of Holy Communion from the Parish Eucharist on the Sunday morning, sharing with them some of the prayers and readings for the day.

There are many opportunities for ministry, and for sharing the joy of ministry among the whole congregation. The full-time paid priest will have a very demanding, but different style of ministry in such a congregation, as a sort of mini-bishop. The diocesan bishop has the authority for doing every aspect of ministry in his diocese, but this he shares with the clergy and lay officials, saying as he does to incumbents at their institution 'Receive the cure of souls which is both yours and mine.' Perhaps in the future, stipendiary clergy will have a task as leaders of the Church, trainers of the ministry, giving oversight, encouragement, leadership but delegating, sharing and learning with the whole church membership.

CELLS

In places where Christians are being led to see the importance of the Cell or House Church, the need will be for more priests to serve their needs than we have now. The model for most priests may well become nearer to the medieval village priest who farmed his glebe and knew as much about swine fever as the next man, than to the 18th century image of the man aloof from the concerns of ordinary mortals, immersed simply in the problems of sacred study. The office worker, postman, policeman or teacher, called trained and ordained to priestly ministry in the Church, sharing the pressures and insecurities of life with everyone else, yet leading a small group of fellow Christians in a sacramental fellowship of prayer, worship, community, and service, may well be a common pattern of church life in the future. He will fulfil perhaps only the liturgical function, and other members of that group will take the lead in teaching, counselling, pastoral care and so on, each having been called, trained and commissioned to their respective spheres of ministry.

Such cells may focus on a residential neighbourhood or a tiny village community, or may have as their common focus the life in a works, a college, the commercial or political life of an inner city, or in a leisure centre such as a regular caravan and camp site, a yachting marina, a hiking centre or youth club. The Christian cell can develop and be serviced wherever people gather for whatever reason, and they do not have to be tied down to the neighbourhood in which people live.

Such irregular Christian activity will of course need careful fostering and nurturing, and there will be a need for some clergy in each diocese to have as their particular ministry the oversight, training and ministry to Cells whose focus is not the place in which they live but their place of their work, or community service, or their leisure. The Bishop of Winchester's little pamphlet *A Church Reshaped* (published by C.M.S., 15p) offers three models of cellular church life which may be significant pointers to the future pattern of Christian community life and ministry.

TRAINING PROGRAMME

35. If we Christians are to be equipped to witness to our faith in the different aspects of our daily lives, then clearly the whole concept of Christian education and training needs thoroughly re-examining. How well prepared, planned and presented is the teaching in our local church? Is it a bit hit and miss, hurriedly prepared the night before, and unsystematic in the over-all training it gives to church members? Is it a chore that the priest who may be very good at liturgy, or counselling, or pastoral work, or administration finds a real burden to him? Is it a task that others beside the clergy can share in?

The whole congregation should expect that at certain periods in the year, the balance of singing, recitation and exhortation in the first part of the Parish Eucharist will be altered to give time for a series of specific teaching sessions on aspects of Christian life and practice, perhaps taking one of the ten themes of the Common Discipline as the focus. This may well be a shared exercise in which members of the congregation participate in presenting to their fellows experiences, mistakes, opportunities and challenges in which they see the Christian faith has a distinctive contribution to make in human affairs. A series of expository sermons, with everyone having the relevant Bible passage in front of them (either from their own Bibles, on a duplicated paper, or a Good News for Modern Man version of one of the books of the Bible) may bring alive the background, the message and the relevance of a particular book to the congregation in a way they have never seen before.

Teaching and practice in ways of praying, an examination from concrete examples of tensions and strains in family life, and perhaps two members of the congregation who see the same problem differently may help to present two possible lines of thought from which members of the congregation can form their own judgement. Perhaps members can bring forward particular ethical issues from work, present them to the congregation, asking for guidance and prayer. In this way maybe other members may become more sensitive to the pressures and conflicts their fellow members face.

The Christian training programme can also be developed through the groups and cells who prepare the liturgy (see p. 105) and through Catechism Groups (p. 116). My own Church Council recently asked for Christian Evening Classes to refresh their minds on basic church teaching which they have not had as a systematic series since their confirmation classes many years ago. People are interested to know of the background to the Bible, how the books came to be written, and the modern developments in archeology and scholarship which throw much more light on the context, political and social background, and theological significance of Biblical concepts which merely appear strange to us today when they leap out at us from the short readings at the Eucharist.

At Ormesby we have found valuable too the Sunday evening programme of 'Subjects for Sunday' when we have raised local community issues and invited into our church local councillors, pressure group members, and government employees to explore subjects of concern and try to relate theological issues to them. Issues of work, the role of the trades unions, community service, health care and preventive community medicine are all subjects we hope in time to explore in this way.

36. *The church can also have a role in public relations, raising issues and relating theological themes to them. Through press releases, feature articles, radio interviews, and duplicated 'Discussion Papers' we can try to prod people in the community to think a little more deeply about where society is drifting, and trying to initiate a debate on values, aims and ideals in our local community life. The training programme in a church should never be just an introverted exercise cultivating the interests of the religiously inclined, but a real attempt to relate the ideals and principles of the Bible to the rough and tumble of life as we know it and live it. In doing so we need to involve people who do not share our convictions so that we may learn from them, and hopefully they may learn from us.*

37. *We must also encourage our local Library to stock Christian books which may help our training programme, and provide source material for those of our members who wish to persue the subject further. By deliberately ordering new or important Christian books, and recommending them in church and in our literature, we can use the County Library service to good effect in our Christian training programme.*

Where we provide a course for church members who feel called to serve in pastoral care or counselling, we should readily seek the wise experience and training of organisations like the Samaritans and Marriage

Guidance if they are able and willing to help. We may well find that while some of our members exercise their ministry within the congregation, many will from such experience be willing to offer their services to those organisations.

There are of course concerns beyond the local neighbourhood which the church can, and does take up. Christians identify themselves with the struggle of people everywhere for freedom, justice and a fair share of the world's resources. The Bishop of Winchester's book *Enough is Enough* (S.C.M. Press, 80p) and F. E. Schumacher's *Small is Beautiful* (Abascus, 75p) point to a long-term philosophy of self-restraint, justice, and a more human way of living, working and sharing the world's resources. These are subjects which have found their way into many parish discussion groups. So too have other ethical issues like abortion, euthanasia, war, crime and punishment, and concerns like pollution and the environment, devolution of power to Scotland, Wales and the English regions. Abroad Christian discussion groups explore their own burning national issues like draft dodging in the United States during the Viet Nam War, or the actions of the Governor-General of Australia in ousting Prime Minister Gough Whitlam.

No one church can hope to cover the whole range of human concerns. Some people feel particularly strongly about certain issues and it will be right to encourage their zeal, and hope to see some concrete action taken from your own local church in furthering Christian concern for the brotherhood of mankind. The important thing is to try conscientiously to relate our Christian vision of life as it could be to the problems of the neighbourhood or the world now, and see what practical steps we can take to help forward the Christian vision. We must not allow ourselves to be over-burdened with guilt by all the possible causes for concern that we cannot tackle.

In considering our church training programme we should expect to learn from our partners in mission in other lands. Christians in Holland (p. 106), Alaska (p. 116) and India (p. 111), as well as many other parts of the world all have experiences of Christian life and ministry in different situations which demand fresh thinking and a willingness to be flexible in relating the unchanging principles of God to the very widely differing circumstances of human life in different parts of our globe. Whereas in England church membership is declining, in Africa and South America it is growing rapidly. We have much to learn from our fellow Christians in other lands.

FELLOWSHIP

Personally I think it is a mistake for any church to provide only one standard type of Christian fellowship activity. Human beings are different, and there is no reason why we should expect everyone to like the same things. The Mothers' Union gatherings provide an important means of fellowship, training and service for some people whereas a different style of activity, for younger people or married couples will appeal to other people. The harvest supper will appeal to some and not others, and so too will fellowship activities like a theatre trip, a dinner/dance, a disco, a Barn Dance, a Country and Western Evening, an evening tour ending with a pub basket meal. As long as we aim in the variety of our social activities to make available (for those who would like that sort of thing) a choice of events so that no large group of people within the Christian community feel they are never catered for, then there is no reason why we should not try in our social activities to break away from the impression of only catering for the cocktail party set, or only for the soggy sandwich and butterfly cake set.

The small local fellowship group, linking fellow church members who live near to each other, is one way of mixing people irrespective of culture and tastes, but those who have a common feeling for things they enjoy should be able to find a means of sharing this with fellow church members even if the majority do not wish to participate.

BISHOPS

It seems to me that the role of the Bishop is crucial in helping local churches to face the opportunities of answering the Archbishops' Call to the Neighbourhood and Nation. Many clergy feel isolated and threatened in their parishes, and feel remote from their bishop. They may have very friendly relationships with the bishop on casual meetings on formal occasions like a confirmation, institution or synod meeting, but rarely have the opportunity for a full and free exchange of views and experiences with their bishop. Often they feel the bishop simply does not fully understand the pressures under which they labour, and so suggestions of embarking on patterns of work that break new ground and depart from traditional practices are often met with discouragement from the bishop. I find it very sad (particularly as I have such a happy relationship with my own suffragan bishop) that in contacts and correspondence with clergy I find similar complaints of remoteness of the bishop from his clergy in different parts of England and Wales, and coming too from America and Australia.

38. *It would be good to see bishops initiating a regular pattern of wide ranging discussions with their clergy in which a reasonable number of priests at a time—say those from two or three deaneries—meet with the bishop. These meetings, twice a year for a full day, could be a valuable means of talking over informally two or three different major subjects each time. In the exchange the bishop can explain his own pressures and frustrations, which his priests may not be aware of, and he can hear ours. The meetings, free from the straight-jacket of synod standing orders, can explore together aspects of Christian training, baptismal discipline, church management, and the role of the local church in society.*

It can be a venue for exchanging valuable ideas, and encouraging experiments and reporting back on them. It can be a mutual learning experience, and one that builds a stronger bond of trust and appreciation between a bishop and his clergy.

LEARNING FROM OTHERS

39. *There is great value in the cross fertilisation of ideas and experience between people of different disciplines and professions. A lot can be learnt from some of the management training and thinking which is available in British commerce and industry. All clergy can profitably learn, adopt and adapt quite a bit of the skills in management and personal relationships which professional managers have to learn. A business works very much on the quality of good personal relationships, communication, and clear objectives for which managers set the tone.*

All clergy whether a bishop in his diocese or a priest in his parish can learn much about improving his role as a pastor, teacher, communicator, and leader from modern management thinking. I belong to the British Institute of Management and find from their publications and meetings a great deal of valuable thinking and practise in the skills of parish management and personal relationships. The skills of management in our church need improving. Bright schemes develop and are soon lost in thin air; the morale of many clergymen is low (and that is a prime responsibility for any man in senior management, the morale of his lower grades of managers); and there is much flag waving among top people, to no great purpose.

Recently a senior Probation Officer told me of a meeting of social workers with a bishop. The bishop had asked to meet them. The meeting was in a pub at lunchtime, it was very pleasant, but none of them afterwards could see the purpose of it. It was no more than a jolly small-talk party. There was no real desire to understand the jobs of the social workers, the difficulties they faced, or explore the ways in which the bishop or local churches could in any way help to alleviate distress and move towards the sort of society we want to create. There was no discussion on the Christian vision of man, and the particular Christian alternative to the current assumptions which deny the reality of sin in people's lives, and do not see any creative value in suffering, repentance and 'new birth'. Too often such 'flag-flying' ventures are wasting everyone's time, but more importantly wasting a valuable opportunity to learn, to understand and to share. I fear that on such occasions the flag that is flying does not represent a kingdom being won but a cause being lost.

I would like to see bishops really hammering out with clergy the needs of the moment in priorities and objectives for Christian life, and encouraging experiments and innovations. The bishop has a responsibility to safeguard the faith, not necessarily the traditional ways of living and expressing that faith. There is great danger in small groups of Christians setting themselves up as independent Christian groups, out of touch with others, and then drifting away from Christian orthodoxy. The bishop, in his role as teacher of the faith, can encourage and help many Christians to explore these ways of meeting, and stress the value, indeed the necessity, of the closest possible ties through a local church and through him with the world-wide church of Christ.

Where clergy and/or laity are reluctant to explore new ways (or old ways polished bright again after being out of fashion in recent years) the bishop can teach, encourage and guide. Only if he has really close bonds of mutual respect and understanding with the local church will he achieve as much as possible.

40. *It would be good if each parish had to send to the bishop each year a statement of their purpose, and their pattern of work in the past year and their hopes for the future. These could be discussed in a personal meeting of the incumbent and a couple of*

lay representatives with the bishop. That may be asking for the moon, but it must clearly be a cause for concern that so many bishops simply do not know what is going on in most of their parishes, and never really talk seriously about parish policy and aims, frustrations and opportunities, progress and setbacks, with representatives from individual parishes.

It would also be good to see the bishops resuming their role as teachers and trainers, holding from time to time courses of teaching and training for clergy and lay leaders in a convenient centre in one part of their diocese. A bishop's Lent course, in which he can give some sytematic teaching would be very valuable, rather than him just dropping pearls of wisdom one at a time in sermons and speeches in widely differing venues. Though more use could be made of these if the bishop was able and willing to duplicate notes or discussion papers on his sermon at an institution, or confirmation or other occasions. Then the local church would be left with something to really talk about after his visit, and something which can be handed on to local press so that the wider community outside the church building can know what he said in their neighbourhood. Some bishops' sermons at confirmations or institutions would make valuable discussion group material in that parish, or provide follow up for the confirmation class in post-confirmation training, or an agenda for the P.C.C. in the weeks following the institution of the new incumbent. Indeed copies of the theme of the confirmation sermon would carry his words far afield to relatives and friends of those confirmed, and as a momento of the occasion to the confirmand, might be treasured and referred to many times in the future.

THE ARCHBISHOPS' QUESTIONS

The real response to the Archbishops' two questions will come from local neighbourhood communities, and the local church can play an essential part in fostering that debate and seeing the resulting action.

Leadership, stimulation and encouragement are vital here, and to provide this we look to lay leaders, the parish clergy and the bishop. The quality of leadership is important, and the willingness to explore different ways of being the Church and doing the Church's work is equally important. If we seek a national repentance—a metanoia, a new direction—we must look for it first in the life of the Church. It will not come by the circulation of hot air or printed pamphlets, but by prayer, careful thought and determined action. The leadership of lay people, priests and bishops is all of crucial importance, and the much needed change of direction is only likely to begin if all three groups of leaders recognise the need of a new direction beginning in themselves.

8

GETTING IT STARTED

I said in the Introduction (p. 13) that in trying to answer the Archbishops' two questions, we must go a step further and answer a third:

> How do we achieve the sort of society we want?

I offer now a group study course for a Lent series, or Bible Class, House Group, Christian Cell or whatever to lead to action in response to the Archbishops.

TO MOVE MOUNTAINS

1. You have to want to move mountains. To hope someone else will move them for you is no good. If you want to create a better society, you have to accept it is possible only if you and a group of others intend to make some constructive beginning.

2. You have to believe it is possible to do so. You may be ploughing a lonely furrow for a long time. You may be out of step with other people in your neighbourhood. But determined action, arising from strongly held convictions, can create changes in society.

3. You have to have a determination to achieve something specific. A vague waffling generalised desire to improve things in general is no good. You have to set a particular target to achieve, and set to on what may be a narrow issue. It will be at the moment, but should also be part of a wider and longer-term strategy.

4. You have to decide what is best to do, what the priorities are, and what you can hope to achieve given the difficulties of the situation which faces you, and the limits of your own abilities and lack of confidence,

and the limitations of the fellow members of your group. Be realistic—but still be ambitious.

Gather a group which meet regularly. Ideally everyone in the group should have read this book. It will be best for all to accept a common commitment to meet eight times as a minimum, for about an hour and a half each time if possible.

Every member should also accept a commitment to talk about the ideas and issues raised in the group with someone at work, someone at home, and some neighbour, none of whom belong to the group. In this way the discussions will continually be earthed in what other people really do think, and not what the group members think they think.

Session One

Make sure everyone knows each other.

Discuss the Introduction (p. 13.)

(a) Do you all agree with the second and third paragraphs?

(b) What sort of society do we want?

(c) What sort of people do we need to be to achieve it?

(d) How do we achieve the sort of society we want?

(e) Does everyone need a philosophy of life which provides us with a frame of reference against which we can check the sort of society to aim for?

Remember to discuss the points raised, some you agree with and some you don't, with at least three people outside the group (someone at work, in the family or circle of friends, a neighbour) between this meeting and the next, so that you can report back some of their comments. Ask them what they think.

Session Two

Someone should quickly summarise the main points made last time, and group members report on their conversations with other people outside the group.

Discuss The Problems of Progress (page 17). Choose only a couple of these questions to discuss.

(a) Are we seeking a big change in society, or lots of small ones?

(b) Is it true in your experience that in Britain now we suffer from spiritual poverty rather than physical poverty? Have we got the Midas touch?

(c) Is moral neutrality healthy? (p. 23).

(d) Is the persuit of prosperity and pleasure often at the expense of children's long term welfare in family life?

(e) Is the size of organisations a real problem in your experience?

(f) Do we need religion to shape the society and civilisation of the future? pp. 28–9).

Remember to discuss the points raised with the same three people as last time. Maybe their interest in the subjects will grow. Ask them what they think, so that again you can report back.

Session Three
Someone should quickly summarise the main points made last time, and group members report on their conversations with other people outside the group.

Then divide the session into four parts, to look fairly superficially at each of the main subjects covered in the next four chapters. The purpose of this is not to explore each one fully, but to see from the main interests and concerns of the members of this particular group, which one of these four subjects they wish to explore in the next three sessions.

(a) *Education and Family Life.* Is the purpose of education something we are really concerned about? Is there a desire within this group to explore views and attitudes on education, religion and school, re-examine our baptism practises, and/or the patterns of celebration and discipline which Christian parents can share with their children at home and at church?

(b) *Work and Relationships.* Has the group got a varied membership of people who work in different jobs? Who belongs to a trade union or professional group? This is a subject which can only be explored when at least half the membership of the group has day-to-day involvement with paid work. A group that consists almost entirely of retired people, housewives, and teenagers are just not sufficiently in touch themselves with this subject to have anything constructive to contribute on it.

(c) *Health and Wholeness.* What do members think is the major cause of illness? Does healthiness lie in the quality of life in the home and community? Have the group members day-to-day contact with problems of sickness? What do you think is the contribution of spirituality to health?

(d) *Community and Faith.* Have you got a lack of neighbourhood community life in your area? Do you think the Church can make a distinctive contribution to healthier and happier community life? Are you interested in exploring ways in which the Church can truly be yeast in the community dough?

The group should then decide which one, and only one, of these four subjects they intend to explore more fully in the next three sessions.

It will perhaps be helpful to have a quiet time of 5–10 minutes, waiting upon God, seeking the guidance of God in making your decision.

When the decision is made, the members should be asked to pray for each other daily, and for God's guidance and blessing on their work together, and praying about the subject they have agreed to explore in the next three sessions.

The members should also be reminded before they leave of the importance of talking again about the issues raised at this meeting with the same three people with whom they discussed the previous subjects raised.

The intention at future meetings will not be to do block reporting back on these, but to make a point of feeding in these outside views during the course of the discussions whenever they seem relevant.

ALTERNATIVES

EDUCATION AND FAMILY LIFE

Session Four: Education and Family Life
- (a) What is the purpose of education? (p. 30).
- (b) Explore the idea of organising a Frontier group on education (p. 31).
- (c) Do you envisage forming one as a practical action to take, following on from the end of this group session? Will you start planning now?
- (d) Where and how should children be taught Christian faith and practise these days?
- (e) Do you agree that if they are to be taught it as a way of life, then it must be taught by those who believe and practise it, and experience of Christian worship must be within a believing community? How can this be done in your neighbourhood?
- (f) How can parents and the Church take up their responsibility, if many local schoolteachers are not Christian believers?

Remember to talk about these subjects with people outside your group.

Session Five: Education and Family Life
- (a) Can we continue to baptise babies in the very different social and cultural climate of Britain today? (pp. 36–9).
- (b) Is it fair to deprive people of the powerful experience of personal response, conscious choice, and the experience of Christian initiation, by doing it to them before they can be aware of what is happening to them?
- (c) Do you think this is important enough to form

a Frontier group on this subject as a follow up to this group exercise? If so, will you begin planning this now, and do you intend to invite a couple of Baptist Christians to join you in the exercise?

Remember to talk about these subjects with people outside your group.

Session Six: Education and Family Life
 (a) What formative experience can we give to our children in family rituals at home at religious festivals? (pp. 40–3). Jewish family life centres a great deal on such activities and this provides a very strong bond, one which both mother and father play crucial roles.
 (b) Can we fight against the greedy materialism of modern Christmas celebrations by introducing in our own families, and perhaps stressing among our fellow church members, ways of celebrating Christmas which puts Christ back in the centre of it?
 (c) Can we explore, as follow up to this group activity, a pattern of home celebration suggestions for many more of our annual festivals, and encourage the weekly family practise of the social meal among all our church families? Perhaps a special group with parents and children of varying ages would find this an interesting and enjoyable exercise to do.

Remember to talk about these subjects with people outside your group.

WORK AND RELATIONSHIPS

Session Four: Work and Relationships
 (a) 'Through the way we live we demonstrate our faith' (p. 45). How do you see this being worked out in your own spheres of work?
 (b) Relationships at work depend much on our view of human beings, and our beliefs (p. 46).

Can we as a group help each other to find the courage and bear the hurt of trying to speak and act on our beliefs in our own jobs? (p. 47)

(c) Will you consider the value of a Frontier Group at, or outside, work to try and understand more objectively one or more current problems, and relate our theology to them? Will you start planning for such a group as a follow-up to this group exercise?

(d) What should be the role of Christians in the politics of work, in trade unions and professional bodies? (pp. 49–51) Are we playing our proper part now, and if not, how shall we begin to do so?

(e) How can we encourage our fellow church members to play their full part in the politics of work?

Remember to talk about these subjects with people outside your group.

Session Five: Work and Relationships

(a) Are you faced with problems of size in the organisation you work for? If so, how can the frustrations and inefficiency be tackled?

(b) Can we do something positive towards making the place in which we work a unit in which human beings have a real chance to be themselves and influence what happens to them? (pp. 52–4).

(c) Can we accept inconsistency? (p. 53).

(d) What is the cost of sin where you work? (p. 55).

(e) How can we tackle the crisis of trust in business? (pp. 54–5).

(f) How can we make at least one specific plan to shift public opinion in our place of work or neighbourhood about attitudes of mind? (pp. 56–7).

Remember to talk about these subjects with people outside your group.

Session Six: Work and Relationships

(a) What can we do in our own locality to help people accept the cut-backs in government services, and the need to re-establish voluntary services? (pp. 57–9).

(b) What attitudes should we begin to encourage in our own area about personal self-discipline, and how can we discourage abuses of the services we all pay taxes for? (pp. 58–9).

(c) 'What can we do about ...?' Are we prepared to take a leaf from the book of those men from Leamington Spa, and act? (p. 60).

(d) What motivates and disciplines people? What makes a person conscientious? (pp. 61–3). How can we do something positive to encourage better attitudes within our own sphere of influence.

(e) Have we any positive suggestions to put forward at work about the creative use of sabbatical leave, work sharing, and reduction of over-time working? (pp. 63–4).

(f) How can we raise low wages locally to end the dilemma of low paid workers that they would be better off unemployed? (pp. 64–5).

'The whole area of work is not some ghetto to be regarded as shut off from the love of God and the insights of Christianity.' 'Clearly this calls the church to re-examine its purpose and priorities in order to help us its members to fulfil ours at work' (p. 65). Do you agree? What are we going to do about it now?

Remember to talk about these subjects with people outside your group.

HEALTH AND WHOLENESS

Session Four: Health and Wholeness

(a) 'Far too often the treatment is not a real search for the social, physical, emotional and spiritual health of a person in the way they live, their personal discipline, their personal relationships

135

and beliefs, but in simply prescribing a chemical substance to alleviate or cure a symptom' (p. 66). Do you agree?

(b) 'Health is a positive quality of well-being.' 'Health is closely linked to political decisions about priorities ... to which resources of money and manpower will be given' (p. 68). Do you agree?

(c) Can we explore in a Frontier group, the whole question of health in our local community? (p. 68). Can we now plan to arrange such a group as a follow up to this course?

(d) What practical steps can we take in our neighbourhood to help the 'key people' (pp. 70–1) to change society's attitudes and values about health?

Remember to talk about these subjects with people outside your group.

Session Five: Health and Wholeness

(a) Read again the Duke of Edinburgh's words (p. 71), and the two paragraphs that follow. Even a few people in a neighbourhood can make a considerable impression on our community's understanding of health and the purpose of life. How can we begin in our neighbourhood?

(b) Can we plan to offer sessions in relaxation and meditation in our area, as a practical follow up to this course? (pp. 72–7).

(c) Counselling and care, sacramental healing and intercession—how can we plan to share these in our neighbourhood?

(d) Do you think it would be a good idea in your church to use simple physical things linked with the Christian festivals to focus healing attitudes and behaviour in our neighbourhood? (pp. 77–8).

Remember to talk about these subjects with people outside your group.

Session Six: Health and Wholeness

(a) Sharing our faith, as part of our search for health, may need some completely fresh thinking about how we do it in our neighbourhood. Consider carefully the value of the creative thinking techniques which management trainers use, and whether they should be tried in your church (p. 79).

(b) Do our services, meetings, fellowship really offer an opportunity for healing relationships, binding up the broken hearted, caring for the poor, the widows and orphans, giving sight to the blind and helping the lame walk? Try and work out one or two new ways in which your church could try to do so more effectively than you do now. Look again at pages 78–81

(c) Will some of the traditional structures and patterns of the churches' work have to be broken for more effective ministry to emerge to meet the demands of the present day? Read again the clergyman's letter on page 83.

Remember to talk about these subjects with people outside your group.

COMMUNITY AND FAITH

Session Four: Community and Faith

(a) Do you agree that the sort of society we want is one that is 'in tune with the Divine Will'? (page 48).

(b) Do you see the liturgy as the focus of all our community concerns? (page 85). Can we take any particular steps to help ourselves and others be involved in it and seeing it as the complete offering to God of all our individual and community concerns?

(c) What do you see as the educational and leadership role that the local church can play in your community? (pp. 120–1) Can you then make some practical plans to put one or more of these into operation in the months following the completion of this course?

Remember to talk about these subjects with people outside your group.

Session Five: Community and Faith
- (*a*) How can we help generate a community enthusiasm for voluntary organisations that provide care, fellowship and entertainment in our neighbourhood?
- (*b*) Can we as individual Christians nourish the formation of local street residents associations? Would this be a worthwhile activity? (pages 87–9).
- (*c*) Should we take any practical steps in our area to use a Christian festival as a cause for public celebration, and sharing Christian teaching in a popular form? (pp. 89 and 92–3)
- (*d*) Should we initiate community conferences or Frontier groups in our neighbourhood? (pages 95–6).

Remember to talk about these subjects with people outside your group.

Session Six: Community and Faith
- (*a*) Will you pray about and consider the value of consciously Christian community life having an influence in your local community, and seek now to know what God is calling you in your church life to do about this? (page 90).
- (*b*) How can we live our faith in the market place of life and really be Christian yeast in the secular dough (page 94) in this parish?
- (*c*) In what practical ways can we, and fellow Christians in our own church and neighbouring churches, begin to set a new ball rolling in our community life that will take us nearer to the sort of society we want, and the sort of people we need to be to achieve it? (pages 95–7).

Remember to talk about these subjects with people outside your group. This practise is important. With the tremendous growth of Christian groups throughout Britain in the past 15 years, the house group movement could well in time have as big an impact in our national life as Robert Raikes did with his Sunday School movement years ago. The activity must lead to closer bonds of love and trust, fellowship and understanding between the members, and lead normally to practical action in our lives. But equally important can be the encouragement it gives to every participant to talk naturally and enthusiastically about the enjoyment and stimulation of belonging to such a group, and using the fact of being at the group meeting to nourish wider conversations in other day to day affairs on the same subjects. It thus makes it possible for every participant to be unselfconsciously a public relations officer for his or her church, and without twisting anybody's arm to come and join us.

Tell whoever you talk to that you belong to the group, and one of the obligations is to ask people outside the group for their opinions on the subjects raised so that the rest of the group can learn what other people think. Most folks then are pleased to listen and comment, and many become very interested in the whole exercise and some want to become involved themselves.

CHURCH AND NEIGHBOURHOOD

Session Seven
(a) The Archbishops have issued a Call to our Nation—do you agree we should see it very much as a Call to our Neighbourhood? (pages 98–9.) and that any neighbourhood, no matter how small, can take action which may become a model for others to want to imitate? (pages 99–100).
(b) Will you have a go at drafting your own statement of the Purpose of your church? (pp. 101–102).

(c) Will you draw up your own practical suggestions for commending and encouraging the practise of prayer in your neighbourhood? (Pages 103–5.)

Remember to talk about these subjects with people outside your group.

Session Eight
(a) Will you begin to plan within your church life to draw up your own Common Discipline? (Pages 111–15).
(b) From this a long-term training programme and strategy is needed for encouraging every member to have a sphere of ministry, and to enjoy the fellowship and encouragement of their fellow Christians (pages 111–19). What plans do you think it right to suggest in your church?
(c) Will you send a report on this exercise to your own bishop, and perhaps invite him to meet you and other members of the congregation at a one-day parish life conference to explore some of the implications of this exercise, and the pattern of relationships you would like to see established between him and the local church? (Pages 123–7).

Remember to talk about these subjects with people outside your group.

This exercise can cover a lot of ground, and clearly offers more than most people will want to tackle. A careful sifting through by Group Leaders can delete parts of it, so that any group tackles what is within their own power to cope with, and their own particular range of interests, and the apparent needs of the local church and community at the present time. A planning group to do this sifting should certainly include lay men and women of different ages and interests, so that the sifting is not simply according to the whims of the parish priest.

The group exercise may cover more than one church, and more than one denomination. This is all to the good in most cases. It is important however that there be proper and full opportunity to report back from the group activity to the wider congregation, so that everyone has a chance of knowing what subjects are being explored, what some of the key issues are, and why it is that church members feel it necessary to take some local community initiatives as a result of this exercise.

Perhaps a Church Life Conference over a weekend will be a good means of drawing some of the key threads together, perhaps moving towards a common acceptance of a Purpose and Common Discipline, and then setting the objectives for so many months ahead, and fixing a report back meeting to see what progress has been made in the months following the study of this book.

Hopefully this will then lead on to a growing vision and sense of achievement in the role of the local church in the neighbourhood and responding to the Archbishops' Call to the Nation, showing that we have some clear ideas of the sort of society we want, and the sort of people we need to be to achieve it, and that we are making some definite efforts to achieve it.

May God bless you in your task.